CONTENTS

CHAPTER 1 WHAT IS THE INSTANT POT AIR FRYER LID?

Functionality And Build

So, in the latter parts of 2019, the IP Company released its newest addition to the family, the Air-Frying Lid, which is impressive for its functionality to air fry, bake, roast, dehydrate, broil, and reheat a wide range of foods.

It is a single lid attachment for the existing instant pot bought separately for added cooking functionality. This means, if you already have a current instant pot, switching into air frying mode will only require replacing the pressure-cooking lid with the air frying one for the new operation. However, the lid caters to this collection of instant pot's; the Duo 60, Duo Plus 60, Lux 60, Ultra 60, Viva 60, Nova Plus 60, Duo Nova 60. The lid will not work with the Smart WiFi 60, Duo Evo Plus 60, Duo Evo Plus 60, Duo SV 60, or Max 60.

Like every other air frying device, the IP version uses a hot air blowing mechanism over foods, which makes them crispy, crusted, baked, or dried after pressure-cooking or not. This method means that you have the option to brown rotisserie chicken after pressure-cooking for that drool-deserving crust. On the other hand, you may kick-off baking some chocolate chip cookies directly with the air frying lid and still turn out with cookies that are crunchy yet melt in your mouth. I genuinely find my possibilities to be endless with the instant pot, and with Easter coming up, I am excited about the many dishes yet to share.

Operation

The reasonably large package of the lid, measuring 13.9 x 12.8 inches and weighing 11.6 pounds may seem bulky for one that could sit a small instant pot. However, you can ascribe the blame to its accompanying accessories that aid with successful air-frying.

In each package contains the air fryer lid, a multi-level air-frying basket, a base for the basket, a dehydrating/broil tray, a protection pad to sit the lid on while it is hot and manual for usage.

Like a traditional air fryer, using the lid requires either positioning food in the air-frying basket or broiling tray to enable it to rotate and cook food evenly using its burner and fan. This process implies that it is not safe to air-fry directly onto the lining of the instant pot. For example, if browning rotisserie chicken, it will be necessary to transfer the food to the air-frying basket before proceeding with browning. Although a little mess to be created, the outcome makes you forget the wipe of extra juice dripped on the counter.

The Various Functions

The decisive moment is here, which is what got everybody curious when we heard the news of the lid's release. What does it do?

The lid caters for six cooking functionalities, all positioned on the lid without any need to adjust any functionality directly on the instant pot. It allows you to air fry, bake, roast, dehydrate, broil, and reheat, and you get to adjust cooking modes, temperature, and time setting all on the lid. Let's look at what each function offers:

Air-fry: Air-frying is a smart way to cut down the use of oils when frying foods with the hot air blowing technique that crisps foods better than deep-frying. This function is ideal for fried chicken, shrimp, crisping vegetables, etc. It uses a default temperature range between 300 F to 400 F, and a cooking time range between 1 minute to 1 hour as the recipe calls. Always use the air-fryer basket for this method.

Bake: Everything bake-able works just as fine with this cooking function from casseroles to desserts. It serves as a mini oven giving you the option to either bake foods in the air fryer basket or introduce a safe accessory like a springform pan. When using the air-fryer basket, make sure to line its inner parts with foil or baking paper before pouring in the batter. On the other hand, if using a safe cake pan, ensure to elevate the pan with a steam rack when cooking. Also, bake without covering except the recipe calls for it. To effect the function, work between a temperature range of 180 F to 380 F and a cooking time range of 1 minute to 1 hour. The ideal tools to use will be the air fryer basket, broil/dehydrating tray, or a safe-oven baking dish.

Roast: Any roast ideas in mind for the weekend? If you've got your lid, then it will be an easier, faster, and more effective turnout. This function is excellent for all roast recipes using pork, beef, poultry, vegetables, lamb, and many types of meats. It creates the perfect crisp and crust on meats and gives vegetables that mouthwatering golden brown exterior. For the right cook, activate the Roast mode on the lid and set the temperature and timing between 250 F and 380 F, and 1 minute and 45 minutes respectively. The right accessories to use are the air fryer basket or broil/dehydrating tray.

Dehydrate: When you find a device that can dehydrate fruits, vegetables, and jerky meats the best, you almost want to give your traditional oven away. That's how I feel with the IP air-fryer lid after churning out the best apple and pear crisps that I have ever made. Using a 105 F to 165 F temperature range and allowing cooking between 1 hour to 72 hours, extraction of juices from foods turns out the best. For dehydrating your pieces, work with the air fryer basket or broil/dehydrating tray for the best results.

Broil: I have tried making French onion soup with the instant pot but always had to introduce a torch to get the right melt and color of Gruyere cheese on the soup after the cook. It is a breeze to use the same air-frying lid for this process with a little adjustment. This broil function creates the best direct-to-heating source browning effect on foods like casseroles, Crème Brulee, etc. by enabling the broiling mode. Place foods directly or indirectly in the air fryer basket or broiling/dehydrating tray, then choose your perfect browning temperature between 180 F and 380 F and cooking time range between 1 minute to 1 hour.

Reheating: While all the instant pot models allow an option to keep food warm after cooking, the air-fryer lid allows for reheating crusted or crisped foods at best. It especially prevents overcooking or over-drying foods, which provides for a temperature range between 120 F to 360 F only and a cooking time range of 1 minute to 1 hour. When reheating foods, make sure to place them in either the air fryer basket, on the broil/dehydrating tray, or a safe-oven baking dish.

Reasons I'm Loving the IP Air-Fryer Lid

It may sound like to early a time to be heavily hooked a new device, and I don't despise that. However, when an invention works so well for its first release, it is always the right place to talk about its goodies. From my side, having used the air-fryer lid these past weeks, I can share a handful of benefits that the equipment has brought to my culinary life. Although I am still exploring and taking notes on its other, not so great elements, let's introduce ourselves to it on the goodness. Shall we begin?

Buy a lid and be good to go!

If you already own an instant pot model that accommodates the air-fryer lid, then that is all you need to have both worlds. You do not need to purchase another device to air-fry, bake, roast, dehydrate, or broil. With a single instant pot and both lids, pressure-cooking and air-frying, cooking for yourself, the family, and everyone else just got seamless.

It is super easy to work with

Like the instant pot, the air-fryer lid only requires a few button pushes here and there, and you are set to make some scrumptious dishes.

It is a thoughtful guide

While cooking with the lid, it will signal you halfway with a beep, and the screen will tell you to flip the food. Now, that is a thoughtful addition to its make to remind you to shake the basket or flip the food just in case your mind wandered off a bit.

It signals you when the lid is placed on correctly

Like the instant pot, a jingle sound is made to inform you that the lid sat on rightly. The air-fryer lid does the same, so you can proceed to apply your functions after that sound.

It allows a good worth of food

The air fryer basket may seem small to the eye but do not be deceived. I comfortably fitted in a good bunch of chicken wings for a six to eight serving size and had a good cook at it.

Maintaining the Air-Fryer Lid for Longevity

It is still a new one out here, so I am still testing ways to use the lid in ways that will keep it around for a very long time. These are my best bet yet:

Avoid electrical damage

Never immerse the lid, its power cord or plug in water or any form of liquid to be cleaned. You stand a chance of damaging the lid and creating electrical shock for yourself.

Use the lid for what it's design

Firstly, never try deep-frying in the instant pot and trying to use the lid over it. While this may sound unheard of, it is still the right place to make a mention.

Secondly, always use the lid with its right accessories and never with the stainless steel insert of the instant pot.

Don't kill two birds with one stone

Never plug the Air-Fryer lid and instant pot cooker base at the same time. You stand a chance of destroying either of the lids or both. Always connect one after the other's use.

Clean the device well

During cooking, grease and food may splatter and build up around the heating element, which could lead to smoke, fire, and personal injury. After each cook and cooling cycle, make sure to clean the lid very thoroughly and leave it to air dry before the next use.

CHAPTER 2: BREAKFAST RECIPES

Breakfast Potatoes

Cooking Time: 25 minutes   Serves: 3

Ingredients:
- Russet potatoes – 1 pound, peeled & cut into ½-inch pieces
- Fresh parsley – 1/2 tbsp., chopped
- Onion powder – ¼ tsp.
- Paprika – ¼ tsp.
- Garlic powder – ¼ tsp.
- Olive oil – 1 ½ tbsps.
- Pepper & salt, to taste

Directions:
1. Add potatoes into the large bowl. Add remaining ingredients over potatoes except for the parsley and toss well. Add potatoes into the multi-level air fryer basket and place basket into the instant pot. Seal pot with air fryer lid. Select bake mode and cook at 380 F for 25 minutes. Stir potatoes halfway through. Garnish with parsley and serve.

Cheesy Breakfast Eggs

Cooking Time: 15 minutes
Serves: 1

Ingredients:
- Eggs – 2
- Parmesan cheese – 1 tbsp., grated
- Cheddar cheese – 2 tbsps., shredded
- Heavy cream – 2 tbsps.
- Pepper & salt, to taste

Directions:
1. Spray one ramekin with cooking spray and set aside. In a small bowl, whisk eggs with heavy cream. Add remaining ingredients and stir well. Pour egg mixture into the prepared ramekin. Place the dehydrating tray into the multi-level air fryer basket and place basket into the instant pot. Place the ramekin on dehydrating tray. Seal pot with the air fryer lid. Select bake mode and cook at 380 F for 15-20 minutes or until eggs are set. Serve.

Breakfast Egg Bite

Cooking Time: 15 minutes
Serves: 8

Ingredients:
- Eggs – 6
- Bacon slices – 3, cooked and crumbled
- Mozzarella cheese – 4 tbsps., shredded
- Cheddar cheese – ½ cup, shredded
- Spinach – ¼ cup, chopped
- Onion – ¼ cup, chopped
- Bell peppers – ½ cup, chopped
- Onions – ¼ cup, chopped
- Heavy cream– 2 tbsps.
- Pepper & salt, to taste

Directions:
1. In a mixing bowl, whisk eggs with heavy cream, pepper, and salt. Add remaining ingredients and stir everything well. Pour egg mixture into the 8 silicone muffin molds. Place the dehydrating tray into the multi-level air fryer basket and place basket into the instant pot. Place the 6 silicone molds on the dehydrating tray. Seal pot with the air fryer lid. Select the air fry mode and cook at 300 F for 15 minutes. Cook the 2 remaining egg bites. Serve.

Banana Breakfast Muffins

Cooking Time: 15 minutes
Serves: 10

Ingredients:
- Ripe bananas – 2, mashed
- Self-raising flour – ¾ cup
- Cinnamon – 1 tsp.
- Vanilla – 1 tsp.
- Brown sugar – ½ cup
- Egg – 1
- Olive oil – 1/3 cup

Directions:
1. In a mixing bowl, beat egg, vanilla, oil, brown sugar, and mashed bananas until combined well. Add flour and cinnamon and mix until combined well. Pour mixture into the 10 silicone muffin molds. Place the dehydrating tray into the multi-level air fryer basket and place basket into the instant pot. Place 6 muffin molds on the dehydrating tray. Seal pot with the air fryer lid. Select air fry mode and cook at 320 F for 15 minutes. Cook remaining muffins. Serve.

Delicious Roasted Potatoes

Cooking Time: 25 minutes   Serves: 2

Ingredients:
- Baby potatoes – 12 oz, cut into chunks
- Olive oil – 1 tsp.
- Italian seasoning – 1 tsp.
- Pepper & salt, to taste

Directions:
1. Add potatoes into the mixing bowl. Add remaining ingredients and toss well. Add potatoes into the multi-level air fryer basket and place basket into the instant pot. Seal pot with air fryer lid. Select air fry mode and cook at 400 F for 25 minutes. Stir potatoes twice while cooking. Serve.

Almond Flour Donuts

Cooking Time: 25 minutes
Serves: 6

Ingredients:
- Almond flour – 1 cup
- Vanilla – ½ tsp.
- Eggs – 2
- Almond milk – ¼ cup
- Butter – ¼ cup, melted
- Cinnamon – 1 tsp.
- Baking powder – 2 tsps.
- Erythritol – ¼ cup
- Sea salt– 1/8 tsp.

Directions:
1. In a mixing bowl, mix together almond flour, cinnamon, baking powder, sweetener, and salt. In a small bowl, whisk together eggs, vanilla, milk, and butter. Pour egg mixture into the almond flour mixture and mix until well combined. Pour batter into the 6 silicone donut molds. Place the dehydrating tray into the multi-level air fryer basket and place basket into the instant pot. Place 4 donut molds on dehydrating tray. Seal pot with air fryer lid. Select bake mode and cook at 350 F for 25 minutes. Cook remaining donuts. Serve.

Vegetable Egg Muffins

Cooking Time: 25 minutes
Serves: 12

Ingredients:
- Mixed vegetables – 3 cups
- Parmesan cheese – 4 tbsps., grated
- Cheddar cheese – 1 cup, shredded
- Onion – 3 tbsps., minced
- Mustard powder – ½ tsp.
- Milk – ¼ cup
- Eggs – 12
- Olive oil – 1 tsp.
- Pepper & salt, to taste

Directions:
1. Cook mixed vegetables in a pan with 1 tsp olive oil until tender. Remove from heat and set aside. In a mixing bowl, whisk eggs with seasonings, and milk. Add remaining ingredients and mix until well combined. Pour egg mixture into the 12 silicone muffin molds. Place the dehydrating tray into the multi-level air fryer basket and place basket into the instant pot. Place 6 muffin molds on dehydrating tray. Seal pot with air fryer lid. Select bake mode and cook at 350 F for 25 minutes. Cook remaining muffins. Serve.

Chia Oat Muffins

Cooking Time: 15 minutes
Serves: 12

Ingredients:
- Oat flour – 1 ¾ cups
- Chia seeds – 1 tbsp.
- Eggs – 2
- Vanilla – 1 tsp.
- Almond milk – 2 tbsps.
- Fresh lemon juice – 2 tbsps.
- Coconut oil – ½ cup, melted
- Applesauce – ½ cup
- Sugar– ½ cup
- Baking soda– ½ tsp.
- Salt – ½ tsp.

Directions:
1. In a small bowl, mix together all the dry ingredients. In a large bowl, beat eggs with vanilla, milk, lemon juice, oil, applesauce, and sugar until combined thoroughly. Add dry ingredients into the wet ingredients and stir until combined well. Add chia seeds and fold well. Pour batter into the 12 silicone muffin molds. Place the dehydrating tray into the multi-level air fryer basket and place basket into the instant pot. Place 6 muffin molds on dehydrating tray. Seal pot with air fryer lid. Select bake mode and cook at 350 F for 15 minutes. Cook remaining muffins. Serve.

Spinach Tomato Egg Muffins

Cooking Time: 12 minutes   Serves: 12

Ingredients:

- Eggs – 10
- Spinach – 1 cup, chopped
- Tomatoes – 1 cup, diced
- Italian seasoning – ¾ tsp.
- Garlic powder – ½ tsp.
- Pepper & salt, to taste

Directions:

1. In a mixing bowl, whisk eggs with garlic powder, Italian seasoning, pepper, and salt. Add spinach and tomatoes and stir well. Pour egg mixture into the 12 silicone muffin molds. Place the dehydrating tray into the multi-level air fryer basket and place basket into the instant pot. Place 6 muffin molds on the dehydrating tray. Seal pot with the air fryer lid. Select bake mode and cook at 380 F for 12 minutes or until set. Cook the remaining muffins. Serve.

Breakfast Egg Puffs

Cooking Time: 15 minutes   Serves: 4

Ingredients:

- Eggs – 4
- Taco seasoning – 1 tsp.
- Baking powder – ½ tsp.
- Parmesan cheese – 2 tbsps., grated
- Onion – 2 tbsps., minced
- Bell pepper – 1 tbsp., diced
- Small tomato – 1, diced
- Squash puree – ½ cup
- Cornstarch– 1 tbsp.

Directions:

1. Spray 4 ramekins with cooking spray and set aside. In a mixing bowl, whisk eggs with remaining ingredients until well combined. Pour egg mixture into the prepared ramekins. Place the dehydrating tray into the multi-level air fryer basket and place basket into the instant pot. Place ramekins on the dehydrating tray. Seal pot with the air fryer lid. Select bake mode and cook at 380 F for 15 minutes or until set. Serve.

Creamy Mac n Cheese

Cooking Time: 5 minutes
Serves: 8

Ingredients:
- 15 oz elbow macaroni
- 1 cup milk
- 1/2 cup parmesan cheese, shredded
- 1 cup mozzarella cheese, shredded
- 2 cups cheddar cheese, shredded
- 1 tsp garlic powder
- 1 tsp hot pepper sauce
- 2 tbsp butter
- 4 cups vegetable broth
- 1/4 tsp pepper
- 1/2 tsp salt

Directions:
1. Add macaroni, garlic powder, hot sauce, butter, broth, pepper, and salt into the instant pot and stir well.
2. Seal pot with lid and cook on manual high pressure for 5 minutes.
3. Once done then release pressure using the quick-release Directions than open the lid.
4. Add cheese and milk and stir until cheese is melted.
5. Serve and enjoy.

Cherry Risotto

Cooking Time: 10 minutes
Serves: 4

Ingredients:
- 1 1/2 cups arborio rice
- 1/2 cup dried cherries
- 3 cups of milk
- 1 cup apple juice
- 1/3 cup brown sugar
- 1 1/2 tsp cinnamon
- 2 apples, cored and diced
- 2 tbsp butter
- 1/4 tsp salt

Directions:
1. Add butter into the instant pot and set the pot on sauté mode.
2. Add rice and cook for 3-4 minutes.
3. Add brown sugar, spices, apples, milk, and apple juice and stir well.
4. Seal pot with lid and cook on manual high pressure for 6 minutes.
5. Once done then release pressure using the quick-release Directions than open the lid.
6. Stir in dried cherries and serve.

Almond Coconut Risotto

Cooking Time: 5 minutes   Serves: 4

Ingredients:
- 1 cup arborio rice
- 1 cup of coconut milk
- 3 tbsp almonds, sliced and toasted
- 2 tbsp shredded coconut
- 2 cups almond milk
- 1/2 tsp vanilla
- 1/3 cup coconut sugar

Directions:
1. Add coconut and almond milk in instant pot and set the pot on sauté mode.
2. Once the milk begins to boil then add rice and stir well.
3. Seal pot with lid and cook on manual high pressure for 5 minutes.
4. Once done then allow to release pressure naturally then open the lid.
5. Add remaining ingredients and stir well.
6. Serve and enjoy.

Creamy Polenta

Cooking Time: 5 minutes   Serves: 3

Ingredients:
- 1/2 cup polenta
- 1 cup of coconut milk
- 1 cup of water
- 1/2 tbsp butter
- 1/4 tsp salt

Directions:
1. Set instant pot on sauté mode.
2. Add milk, water, and salt in a pot and stir well.
3. Once milk mixture begins to boil then add polenta and stir to combine.
4. Seal pot with lid and cook on high pressure for 5 minutes.
5. Once done then allow to release pressure naturally then open the lid.
6. Stir and serve.

Sweet Cherry Chocolate Oat

Cooking Time: 15 minutes   Serves: 4

Ingredients:
- 2 cups steel cuts oats
- 3 tbsp honey
- 2 cups of water
- 2 cups of milk
- 3 tbsp chocolate chips
- 1 1/2 cups cherries
- 1/4 tsp cinnamon
- Pinch of salt

Directions:
1. Spray instant pot from inside with cooking spray.
2. Add all ingredients into the pot and stir everything well.
3. Seal pot with lid and cook on high pressure for 15 minutes.
4. Once done then allow to release pressure naturally then open the lid.
5. Stir well and serve.

Coconut Lime Breakfast Quinoa

Cooking Time: 1 minute   Serves: 5

Ingredients:
- 1 cup quinoa, rinsed
- 1/2 tsp coconut extract
- 1 lime juice
- 1 lime zest
- 2 cups of coconut milk
- 1 cup of water

Directions:
1. Add all ingredients into the instant pot and stir well.
2. Seal pot with lid and cook on manual high pressure for 1 minute.
3. Once done then allow to release pressure naturally for 10 minutes then release using the quick-release Directions. Open the lid.
4. Stir well and serve.

Quick & Easy Farro

Cooking Time: 10 minutes   Serves: 4

Ingredients:
- 1 cup pearl farro
- 1 tsp olive oil
- 2 cups vegetable broth
- 1/4 tsp salt

Directions:
1. Add all ingredients into the instant pot and stir well.
2. Seal pot with lid and cook on manual mode for 10 minutes.
3. Once done then allow to release pressure naturally for 5 minutes then release using the quick-release Directions. Open the lid.
4. Stir well and serve.

CHAPTER 3: BEEF,PORK AND LAMB RECIPES

Flavorful Crispy Crust Pork Chops

Cooking Time: 17 minutes
Serves: 2

Ingredients:
- Pork chops – 2, bone-in
- Onion powder – 1/2 tsp.
- Paprika – 1/2 tsp.
- Parsley – 1/2 tsp.
- Olive oil – 1 tbsp.
- Pork rinds – 1 cup, crushed
- Garlic powder – 1/2 tsp.

Directions:
1. In a bowl, mix together pork rinds, garlic powder, onion powder, paprika, and parsley. Brush pork chops with oil and coat with pork rind mixture. Place coated pork chops into the multi-level air fryer basket and place the basket into the instant pot. Seal pot with the air fryer lid. Select air fry mode and cook at 400 F for 12 minutes. Turn pork chops and air fry for 5 minutes more. Serve.

Easy Ranch Pork Chops

Cooking Time: 35 minutes   Serves: 4

Ingredients:
- Pork chops – 4, boneless
- Olive oil – 4 tbsp.
- Ranch seasoning – 1 1/2 tbsps.

Directions:
1. Mix together ranch seasoning and olive oil and rub over pork chops. Place pork chops into the multi-level air fryer basket and place basket into the instant pot. Seal pot with the air fryer lid. Select Bake mode and cook at 380 F for 35 minutes. Turn pork chops halfway through. Serve.

Breaded Pork Chops

Cooking Time: 35 minutes   Serves: 4

Ingredients:
- Pork chops – 2, boneless
- Paprika – 1/8 tsp.
- Breadcrumbs – 2 tbsps.
- Parmesan cheese – 1/3 cup, grated
- Olive oil – 1 tbsp.
- Garlic powder – 1/4 tsp.
- Dried parsley – 1/2 tsp.
- Pepper & salt, to taste

Directions:
1. Brush pork chops with olive oil. In a shallow bowl, mix together breadcrumbs, cheese, paprika, parsley, garlic powder, pepper, and salt. Coat pork chops with breadcrumb mixture and place into the multi-level air fryer basket and place the basket into the instant pot. Seal pot with the air fryer lid. Select Bake mode and cook at 350 F for 35 minutes. Turn pork chops halfway through. Serve.

Buttery Pork Chops

Cooking Time: 15 minutes   Serves: 2

Ingredients:
- Pork chops – 2
- Butter –4 tbsps., melted
- Garlic cloves – 2, minced
- Thyme – 1 tbsp., chopped
- Pepper & salt, to taste

Directions:
1. Season pork chops with pepper and salt. Mix together butter, thyme, and garlic and brush over pork chops. Place pork chops into the multi-level air fryer basket and place the basket into the instant pot. Seal pot with the air fryer lid. Select Bake mode and cook at 375 F for 15 minutes. Serve.

Moist & Juicy Pork Chops

Cooking Time: 18 minutes   Serves: 2

Ingredients:
- Pork chops – 2, boneless
- Garlic powder – 1 tsp.
- Onion powder – 1 tsp.
- Paprika – 1/2 tbsp
- Olive oil – 1 tbsp.
- Oregano – 1/2 tbsp.
- Pepper & salt, to taste

Directions:
1. Brush pork chops with oil. Mix together oregano, garlic powder, onion powder, paprika, pepper, and salt and rub all over pork chops. Place pork chops into the multi-level air fryer basket and place the basket into the instant pot. Seal pot with the air fryer lid. Select Bake mode and cook at 380 F for 18 minutes. Turn pork chops halfway through. Serve.

Tender Pork Chops

Cooking Time: 15 minutes   Serves: 4

Ingredients:
- Pork chops – 4, boneless
- Olive oil – 4 tbsps.
- Onion powder – 1 tsp.
- Paprika – 1 tsp.
- Pepper & salt, to taste

Directions:
1. Brush pork chops with oil. Mix together onion powder, paprika, pepper, and salt and rub over pork chops. Place pork chops into the multi-level air fryer basket and place the basket into the instant pot. Seal pot with air fryer lid. Select Bake mode and cook at 380 F for 15 minutes. Turn pork chops halfway through. Serve.

Parmesan Crisp Pork Chops

Cooking Time: 30 minutes   Serves: 3

Ingredients:
- Pork chops – 3, boneless
- Milk – 2 tbsps.
- Egg –1, lightly beaten
- Parmesan cheese – 3 tbsps.,
- grated
- Crackers – 1/2 cup, crushed
- Pepper & salt, to taste

Directions:
1. In a shallow bowl, whisk egg and milk. In a separate shallow bowl, mix together cheese, crushed crackers, pepper, and salt. Dip pork chops in egg then coat with cheese mixture and place into the multi-level air fryer basket and place the basket into the instant pot. Seal pot with the air fryer lid. Select Bake mode and cook at 350 F for 30 minutes. Turn pork chops halfway through. Serve.

Sweet Potato Steak

Cooking Time: 32-35 minutes
Serves: 5

Ingredients:
- 2 teaspoons black pepper
- 1 tablespoon maple syrup
- 2 large sweet potatoes, peeled & cubed
- 1/2 cup beef broth
- 1 cup water
- 1/2 pound turkey bacon, sliced
- 2 tablespoons parsley
- 2 tablespoons thyme
- 1 tablespoon olive oil
- 5 carrots. make sticks
- 1 large red onion, sliced
- 1 pound flank steak
- 2 teaspoons rock salt
- 2 cloves garlic minced

Directions:
1. Pat dry the beef and season it.
2. Arrange your Instant Pot over a dry, clean platform. Plug it in power socket and turn it on.
3. Now press "Saute" mode from available options. In the cooking area, add the oil and beef; cook to brown evenly.
4. Add the onion, turkey bacon and other ingredients.
5. Close the lid and lock. Ensure that you have sealed the valve to avoid leakage.
6. Press "Manual" mode from available cooking settings and set cooking time to 25 minutes. Instant Pot will start cooking the ingredients after a few minutes.
7. After the timer reads zero, press "Cancel" and quick release pressure.
8. Carefully remove the lid and serve the prepared keto dish warm!

Garlic Roast

Cooking Time: 40-45 minutes
Serves: 8-10

Ingredients:
- ½ cup onion, chopped
- 2 cups water
- ¼ teaspoon xanthan gum
- 1 teaspoon garlic powder
- 3-pound chuck roast, boneless
- ¼ cup balsamic vinegar
- Parsley, chopped to garnish
- 1 teaspoon pepper
- 1 tablespoon kosher salt

Directions:
1. Slice your roast in half and season with the garlic, pepper, and salt.
2. Arrange your Instant Pot over a dry, clean platform. Plug it in power socket and turn it on.
3. Now press "Saute" mode from available options. In the cooking area, add the meat; cook to brown.
4. Add the onion, water, and vinegar. Stir gently.
5. Close the lid and lock. Ensure that you have sealed the valve to avoid leakage.
6. Press "Manual" mode from available cooking settings and set cooking time to 35 minutes. Instant Pot will start cooking the ingredients after a few minutes.
7. After the timer reads zero, press "Cancel" and quick release pressure.
8. Carefully remove the lid. Carefully take the meat and make chunks.
9. Set the pot back on sauté; boil the mix for around 10 minutes.
10. Mix the gum and mix the shredded meat. Serve the prepared keto dish warm!

Milky Beef Roast

Cooking Time: 30 minutes
Serves: 7-8

Ingredients:
- 1 tablespoon paprika
- 2-pounds beef roast
- 1 cup almond milk
- 1 teaspoon salt
- 1 teaspoon raw honey

Directions:
1. Combine the almond milk and salt in a mixing bowl. Add the paprika and raw honey. Stir the mixture well; add the beef roast in the almond milk mixture and leave for 15 minutes.
2. Take your Instant Pot; open the top lid. Plug it and turn it on.
3. In the cooking pot area, add the bowl mix. Using a spatula, stir the ingredients.
4. Close the top lid and seal its valve.
5. Press "MANUAL" setting. Adjust cooking time to 30 minutes.
6. Allow the recipe to cook for the set cooking time.
7. After the set cooking time ends, press "CANCEL" and then press "QPR (Quick Pressure Release)".
8. Instant Pot will quickly release the pressure.
9. Open the top lid, add the cooked recipe mix in serving plates.
10. Serve and enjoy!

Beef Avocado Bowl

Cooking Time: 10-12 minutes
Serves: 4

Ingredients:
- 2 teaspoons lime juice
- 1 tablespoon olive oil, extra virgin
- 1/2 teaspoon cracked pepper
- 1/2 teaspoon sea salt
- 1/2 teaspoon chili powder
- 2 pounds beef steak strips
- 1 garlic clove, minced
- 1 tablespoon water
- 3 avocado, diced

Directions:
1. Arrange your Instant Pot over a dry, clean platform. Plug it in power socket and turn it on.
2. Now press "Saute" mode from available options. In the cooking area, add the oil and garlic; cook for 1-2 minutes to soften.
3. Add water, lime juice, sea salt, chili powder, and pepper; stir gently.
4. Close the lid and lock. Ensure that you have sealed the valve to avoid leakage.
5. Press "Manual" mode from available cooking settings and set cooking time to 10 minutes. Instant Pot will start cooking the ingredients after a few minutes.
6. After the timer reads zero, press "Cancel" and quick release pressure. Carefully remove the lid.
7. Press "Sauté" button, add the steak strips and stir and cook for 2 minutes.
8. Continue sautéing until chili becomes thicker and reduced by half size. Top with diced avocados.

Broccoli Beef with Garlic Twist

Cooking Time: 20 minutes

Serves: 5

Ingredients:
- 1/2 cup poultry broth
- 1/8 teaspoon salt
- 1 pound cooked beef
- 2 teaspoons garlic, crushed
- 1 tablespoon animal fat
- 6 cups broccoli, cut to prepare small florets
- 1 onion, chopped
- 1 turnip, chopped

Directions:
1. Arrange your Instant Pot over a dry, clean platform. Plug it in power socket and turn it on.
2. Open the lid from the top and put it aside; add the mentioned ingredients and gently stir them.
3. Close the lid and lock. Ensure that you have sealed the valve to avoid leakage.
4. Press "Manual" mode from available cooking settings and set cooking time to 20 minutes. Instant Pot will start cooking the ingredients after a few minutes.
5. After the timer reads zero, press "Cancel" and quick release pressure.
6. Carefully remove the lid and serve the prepared keto dish warm!

Beef Broccoli Curry

Cooking Time: 45 minutes
Serves: 6

Ingredients:
- 1/2 pound broccoli florets
- 2 tablespoons curry powder
- 14 ounces coconut milk
- Salt as needed
- 2 1/2 pound beef stew chunks, small cubes
- 2 medium zucchinis, chopped
- ½ cup water or chicken broth
- 1 tablespoon garlic powder

Directions:
1. Arrange your Instant Pot over a dry, clean platform. Plug it in power socket and turn it on.
2. Open the lid from the top and put it aside; add the ingredients and gently stir them.
3. Close the lid and lock. Ensure that you have sealed the valve to avoid leakage.
4. Press "Manual" mode from available cooking settings and set cooking time to 45 minutes. Instant Pot will start cooking the ingredients after a few minutes.
5. After the timer reads zero, press "Cancel" and quick release pressure.
6. Carefully remove the lid. Add the milk and stir.
7. Add salt as needed and serve the prepared keto dish warm!

Wine Braised Beef Roast

Cooking Time: 48 minutes   Serves: 5-6

Ingredients:
- 2 celery stalks, chopped
- 1 bell pepper, chopped
- 2 tablespoons olive oil
- 2 tablespoons Italian seasoning
- 2 ½ pounds beef roast
- 1 onion, sliced
- 2 garlic cloves, sliced
- 1 cup red wine
- 1 cup beef broth
- 2 tablespoons steak sauce, sugar-free

Directions:
1. Take your Instant Pot; open the top lid. Plug it and turn it on.
2. Press "SAUTÉ" setting and the pot will start heating up.
3. In the cooking pot area, add the meat and half of the oil. Stir and cook for 4-5 minutes until evenly brown from all sides.
4. Set aside in a plate.
5. Heat the remaining olive oil and add the onions, celery, and peppers. Cook for 3 minutes to soften.
6. Stir in the garlic and seasonings and cook for 1 minute. Return the beef to the pot.
7. Add the broth, sauce, and red wine; whisk the mixture.
8. Close the top lid and seal its valve.
9. Press "MANUAL" setting. Adjust cooking time to 40 minutes.
10. Allow the recipe to cook for the set cooking time.
11. After the set cooking time ends, press "CANCEL" and then press "NPR (Natural Pressure Release)".
12. Instant Pot will slowly and naturally release the pressure.
13. Open the top lid, add the cooked recipe mix in serving plates.
14. Serve and enjoy!

Delicious Beef Roast

Cooking Time: 8 hours
Serves: 2

Ingredients:
- 1 lb bottom round roast
- 1/2 tsp oregano, dried
- 1/2 tsp rosemary, crushed
- 1/2 tsp fennel seed
- 1 tsp garlic, sliced
- 1/4 cup water
- 1/4 cup onions, caramelized
- 1/2 tsp pepper
- 1/4 tsp salt

Directions:
1. In a bowl, combine together rosemary, fennel seeds, pepper, oregano, and salt.
2. Rub rosemary mixture all over meat and place in the refrigerator for 30 minutes.
3. Place marinated roast into the inner pot of instant pot duo crisp and top with garlic, onions, and water.
4. Seal the pot with pressure cooking lid and select slow cook mode and cook on low for 8 hours.
5. Remove roast from pot and slice.
6. Serve and enjoy.

Spicy Pulled Beef

Cooking Time: 8 hours
Serves: 6

Ingredients:
- 2 lbs lean beef eye round, trimmed
- 2 tbsp fresh lime juice
- 1 tbsp Worcestershire sauce
- 1 cup can tomato, diced
- 1/4 cup beef broth
- 2 jalapeno peppers
- 1 onion, diced
- 1/4 tsp coriander
- 1/4 tsp oregano
- 1/2 tsp cumin
- 1 tsp garlic, sliced
- 1 red bell pepper, diced

Directions:
1. Season meat with pepper and salt and place into the inner pot of instant pot duo crisp.
2. Add garlic, red pepper, onion, and jalapeno peppers around the beef.
3. Mix together coriander, lime juice, Worcestershire sauce, tomatoes, oregano, cumin, and broth and pour over meat.
4. Seal the pot with pressure cooking lid and select slow cook mode and cook on low for 8 hours.
5. Remove meat from pot and shred using a fork.
6. Return shredded meat to the pot and stir well.
7. Serve and enjoy.

CHAPTER 4: POULTRY RECIPES

Mushroom Turkey Patties

Cooking Time: 10 minutes
Serves: 4

Ingredients:
- Ground turkey – 1 pound
- Breadcrumbs – 4 tbsps.
- Mustard – 1 tsp.
- Worcestershire sauce – 1 tbsp.
- Fresh parsley – 1 tbsp., chopped
- Garlic cloves – 2, minced
- Small onion – 1, minced
- Mushrooms – 4, chopped
- Pepper & salt, to taste

Directions:
1. Add all ingredients into the mixing bowl and mix until combined thoroughly. Make patties and place them in the refrigerator for 30 minutes. Remove turkey patties from the refrigerator and place it into the multi-level air fryer basket. Place the basket into the instant pot. Seal pot with the air fryer lid. Select air fry mode and cook at 330 F for 10 minutes. Serve.

Turkey Meatballs

Cooking Time: 10 minutes   Serves: 4

Ingredients:
- Ground turkey – 1 pound
- Soy sauce – 1 tbsp.
- Fresh parsley – 4 tbsps., chopped
- Egg – 1, lightly beaten
- Breadcrumbs – ½ cup
- Pepper & salt, to taste

Directions:
1. Add all ingredients into the large bowl and mix until combined thoroughly. Make small balls and place them into the multi-level air fryer basket and place basket into the instant pot. Seal pot with the air fryer lid. Select air fry mode and cook at 400 F for 10 minutes. Turn meatballs halfway through. Serve.

Spinach Turkey Patties

Cooking Time: 30 minutes   Serves: 4

Ingredients:
- Ground turkey – 1 pound
- Breadcrumbs – 4 tbsps.
- Mozzarella cheese – 4 oz, shredded
- Dried basil – 2 tsps.
- Dried parsley – 2 tsps.
- Worcestershire sauce – 2 tsps.
- Lemon zest – 1 tsp.
- Vinegar – 2 tbsps.
- Small onion– 1/2, minced
- Spinach– 3 cups
- Olive oil – 2 tbsps.
- Pepper & salt, to taste

Directions:
1. Heat 1 tablespoon of olive oil in a pan over medium heat. Add spinach and sauté until spinach is wilted. Transfer sautéed spinach into the mixing bowl. Add remaining ingredients into the bowl and mix until combined thoroughly. Make patties and place them into the multi-level air fryer basket and place basket into the instant pot. Seal pot with the air fryer lid. Select bake mode and cook at 375 F for 30 minutes. Serve.

Crunchy Japanese Chicken Chop with Katsu Sauce

Cooking Time: 40 minutes
Serves: 4

Ingredients:
- 1 pound boneless skinless chicken breast, sliced in half horizontally
- 2 large eggs
- 1½ cups panko bread crumbs
- Salt and ground black pepper to taste

Katsu Sauce:
- ½ cup ketchup
- 2 teaspoons Worcestershire sauce
- 2 tablespoons soy sauce
- 1 tablespoon sherry
- 1 tablespoon brown sugar
- 1 teaspoon garlic, minced
- Cooking spray

Directions:
1. In a bowl, whisk the eggs. On a plate, pour the bread crumbs.
2. Place the chicken on a clean work surface, and dust with salt and pepper. Dip the chicken pieces in the whisked eggs first, then in bread crumbs to coat well.
3. Spritz the air fryer basket with cooking spray, then arrange the breaded chicken pieces in the basket.
4. Put the air fry lid on and cook in the preheated instant pot at 350°F for 18 minutes or until an instant-read thermometer inserted the center registers at least 165°F. Spray the chicken with cooking spray and flip the chicken pieces when the lid screen indicates 'TURN FOOD' halfway through.
5. Meanwhile, to make the katsu sauce, in a bowl, mix the ketchup, Worcestershire sauce, soy sauce, sherry, brown sugar, and garlic together. Set aside until ready to serve.
6. Remove the chicken from the basket to a platter. Slice into strips and serve with the katsu sauce.

Sweet and Spicy Coconut Chicken with Thai Sauce

Cooking Time: 20 minutes   Serves: 4

Ingredients:
- ½ cup canned coconut milk
- 1 cup sweetened coconut, shredded
- 1 pound boneless skinless chicken breasts, cut into strips
- ½ cup pineapple juice
- 2 tablespoons brown sugar
- 1 teaspoon ground ginger
- 1 tablespoon soy sauce
- 2 teaspoons Sriracha sauce
- 2 eggs
- 1 cup panko bread crumbs
- ½ teaspoon ground black pepper
- 1½ teaspoons salt
- Cooking spray

Directions:
1. In a bowl, combine the coconut milk and pineapple juice. Mix in the brown sugar, ginger, soy sauce, and Sriracha sauce, then add the chicken strips. Cover the bowl in plastic wrap and refrigerate for at least 2 hours or overnight.
2. Before coating, take the chicken strips out of the refrigerator, shake off the excess.
3. In a bowl, whisk the eggs. In another bowl, combine the shredded coconut, bread crumbs, pepper, and salt.
4. Steep the chicken strips in the beaten eggs, then in the coconut mixture, and back into the the beaten egg, and again in coconut mixture.
5. Spritz the air fryer basket with cooking spray. Place the breaded chicken strips in the basket.
6. Put the air fry lid on. Cook in the preheated instant pot at 375°F for 12 minutes, flipping the chicken strips when the lid screen indicates 'TURN FOOD' halfway through or until lightly browned.
7. Remove the chicken from the basket to a platter and serve warm.

Crispy Panko Crusted Chicken Balls

Cooking Time: 55 minutes   Serves: 6

Ingredients:
- 1 package (19-ounce) ground chicken breast
- 1 cup panko bread crumbs
- ½ cup unsalted butter, softened
- 2 cloves garlic, crushed
- 2 tablespoons flat-leaf parsley, chopped
- 2 eggs
- 1 teaspoon paprika
- Salt and ground black pepper, to taste
- Cooking spray

Directions:
1. In a large bowl, combine the butter with garlic and parsley. Divide and spoon 12 equal parts of the mixture on a baking sheet. Refrigerate for 20 minutes or until frozen.
2. Divide the ground chicken into 12 equal sized parts, and press the center of each part to make an indention. Add a spoon of butter mixture into the indention. Wrap the mixture in the ground chicken part and shape it into a ball. Repeat with remaining butter mixture and ground chicken parts. Set aside.
3. Whisk the eggs in a separate bowl. In a third bowl, mix the panko, paprika, black pepper, and salt.
4. Drop each chicken ball in the whisked eggs, then in the panko mixture. Repeat the dredging process for one more time. Shake the excess off. Transfer all balls to a baking sheet; refrigerate for 10 minutes.
5. Spritz the air fryer basket with cooking spray, put the balls in the basket. You may need to work in batches to avoid overcrowding.
6. Put the air fryer lid on and cook in the preheated instant pot at 400°F for 10 minutes. Spritz the balls with cooking spray and turn the balls over when the lid screen indicates 'TURN FOOD' halfway through the cooking time.
7. Remove the chicken balls from the basket. Serve warm with ketchup, if desired.

Bang Bang Chicken with Yogurt Sauce

Cooking Time: 30 minutes
Serves: 4

Ingredients:
- 1 pound boneless, skinless chicken breasts, cut into 1-inch pieces
- 1 egg
- ½ cup milk
- 1 tablespoon hot pepper sauce
- ½ cup flour
- ½ cup tapioca starch
- 1 teaspoon garlic, granulated
- ½ teaspoon cumin
- 1½ teaspoons salt
- Cooking spray

Yogurt Sauce:
- ¼ cup plain Greek yogurt
- 1 teaspoon hot sauce
- 3 tablespoons sweet chili sauce

Directions:
1. In a bowl, whisk the egg, milk, and hot sauce together. In a second bowl, mix the flour, tapioca starch, garlic, cumin, and salt. Set aside.
2. Dredge the chicken pieces in the egg mixture first, then in the flour mixture. Shake off the excess.
3. Spritz the air fryer basket with cooking spray. Arrange them in the basket, and spritz with cooking spray.
4. Put the air fry lid on. Cook in the preheated instant pot at 375°F for 5 minutes, shaking the basket once halfway through or until the chicken is crisp outside and juicy inside.
5. Meanwhile, to make yogurt sauce, in a small bowl, mix the Greek yogurt, hot sauce, and sweet chili sauce.
6. Remove the chicken from the basket and serve with the yogurt sauce on a plate.

Mexican Marinated Turkey Fajitas

Cooking Time: 30 minutes   Serves: 6

Ingredients:
- 1 pound skinless, boneless turkey breast, cut into ½-inch thick slices
- 1 tablespoon chili powder
- 1 teaspoon garlic powder
- ½ teaspoon onion powder
- 1 tablespoon ground cumin
- ½ tablespoon paprika
- 1 teaspoon freshly ground black pepper
- ½ tablespoon dried Mexican oregano
- 2 limes, divided
- 1½ tablespoons vegetable oil, divided
- 1 large red bell pepper, sliced into strips
- 1 large red bell pepper, sliced into strips
- 1 medium yellow bell pepper, sliced into strips
- 1 large red onion, halved and sliced into strips
- 1 jalapeño pepper, deseeded and chopped, or more to taste
- ¼ cup fresh cilantro, chopped

Directions:
1. In a bowl, mix the chili powder, garlic powder, onion powder, cumin, paprika, pepper, and oregano. Set aside.
2. Mist the lime juice over the turkey slices in a separate large bowl, add the seasoning mixture and 1 tablespoon of oil. Toss to coat well. Set aside.
3. In a third bowl, put the bell peppers and onion. Drizzle with the remaining oil. Toss to fully coat. Arrange the bell peppers and onion in the air fryer basket.
4. Put the air fry lid on. Cook in the preheated instant pot at 375°F for 10 minutes. Shake the basket when the lid indicates 'TURN FOOD' halfway through the cooking. Add the jalapeños and cook for 5 minutes more.
5. Put the turkey slices over the vegetables. Cook for 7 to 8 minutes. Flip the chicken halfway through and cook until the the strips are crispy outside and the peppers are tender.
6. Remove the chicken and vegetables from the basket. Serve with cilantro and squeeze juice of remaining lime over.

Air-fried Chicken Kiev

Cooking Time: 40 minutes   Serves: 2

Ingredients:
- 2 (8-ounce) skinless, boneless chicken breast halves, pounded to ¼-inch thickness
- 4 tablespoons butter, softened
- 1 clove garlic, minced
- 2 tablespoons fresh flat-leaf parsley, chopped
- 1 teaspoon salt
- Salt and ground black pepper to taste
- ½ cup all-purpose flour
- 1 egg, beaten
- 1 cup panko bread crumbs
- 1 teaspoon paprika
- Cooking spray

Directions:
1. In a bowl, evenly combine the butter, garlic, parsley, and salt. Half the butter mixture and place on a baking sheet to cool for 10 minutes.
2. On a clean work surface, season the chicken with salt and pepper. Place the halved butter in the center of each chicken breast. Roll the side up to wrap the butter mixture, then wrap them in plastic. Refrigerate for 30 minutes.
3. In a second bowl, combine the flour and beaten egg. In a third bowl, combine the bread crumbs and paprika.
4. Remove the chicken from the refrigerator. Dredge each chicken breast in the second bowl, then in the third bowl.
5. Spritz the air fryer basket with cooking spray, arrange the breaded chicken in the basket.
6. Put the air fry lid on and cook in the preheated instant pot at 400°F for 10 minutes. Spritz the chicken with cooking spray and flip when the lid screen indicates 'TURN FOOD' halfway through.
7. Transfer the cooked chicken to a platter and chill for 5 minutes. Slice to serve.

Pretzel Crusted Chicken Chunks

Cooking Time: 20 minutes
Serves: 6

Ingredients:
- 1½ pound chicken breasts, boneless, skinless, cut into bite-sized chunks
- ½ cup crushed pretzels
- 2 eggs
- 1 teaspoon paprika
- 1 teaspoon shallot powder
- Sea salt and ground black pepper, to taste
- ½ cup vegetable broth
- 3 tablespoons tomato paste
- 3 tablespoons Worcestershire sauce
- 1 tablespoon apple cider vinegar
- 1 tablespoon cornstarch
- 2 tablespoons olive oil
- 1 jalapeño pepper, minced
- 2 garlic cloves, chopped
- 1 teaspoon yellow mustard

Directions:
1. In a large bowl, beat the eggs until frothy and dredge the chicken chunks in it until well coated.
2. Mix the crushed pretzels, paprika, shallot powder, salt, and pepper well in another bowl. And then toss the chicken into the mixture to get a good coating.
3. Arrange the well-coated chunks in the air fryer basket. Put the air fryer lid on and cook in the preheated instant pot at 375°F for 12 minutes, shaking the air fryer basket when it shows 'TURN FOOD' on the lid screen during cooking time.
4. In the meantime, in a third bowl combine the vegetable broth with tomato paste, Worcestershire sauce, apple cider vinegar, and cornstarch.
5. Heat a frying pan over medium-high heat. Add the olive oil, then stir in the jalapeño pepper and garlic, and stir-fry for 30 to 40 seconds.
6. Pour the cornstarch mixture in the pan and bring it to a simmer. Keep stirring. When the sauce starts to thicken, put the air-fired chicken chunks and mustard in. Simmer it for an additional 2 minutes.
7. Transfer them onto a platter and serve. Bon appetit !

Asian Flavor Sticky Chicken Thighs

Cooking Time: 35 minutes
Serves: 6

Ingredients:
- 2 pounds chicken thighs
- 1 tablespoon sesame oil
- ¼ teaspoon paprika
- 1 teaspoon Chinese Five-spice powder
- 1 teaspoon pink Himalayan salt
- 1 tablespoon mustard
- 1 tablespoon sweet chili sauce
- 1 tablespoon rice wine vinegar
- 2 tablespoons soy sauce
- 6 tablespoons honey

Directions:
1. Rub the chicken thighs with sesame oil on all sides. Sprinkle the paprika, Chinese Five-spice powder, and salt over to season.
2. Place the chicken thighs into the air fryer basket. Put the air fryer lid on and cook the thighs in batches in the preheated instant pot at 350°F for 23 minutes. Flip the thighs when the lid screen indicates 'TURN FOOD' halfway through.
3. Meanwhile, heat a pan over medium-high heat, and mix-in the remaining ingredients. Stir the sauce until it reduces by one-third.
4. Put the thighs in the pan, stir carefully until the thighs are coated with the sauce.
5. Transfer them to a platter. Let stand for 10 minutes. Slice to serve.

Rustic Drumsticks with Tamari and Hot Sauce

Cooking Time: 40 minutes
Serves: 6

Ingredients:
- 6 chicken drumsticks
- Nonstick cooking spray
- Sauce:
- ½ teaspoon dried oregano
- 3 tablespoons tamari sauce
- 1 teaspoon dried thyme
- 6 ounces hot sauce

Directions:
1. Spritz the air fryer basket with the nonstick cooking spray. Place the chicken drumsticks in the air fryer basket.
2. Put the air fryer lid on and cook in the preheated instant pot at 375°F for 35 minutes. Spritz the drumsticks with the nonstick cooking spray and flip when the lid screen indicates 'TURN FOOD' halfway through cooking time.
3. Meanwhile, warm a saucepan over medium-low heat, then add oregano, tamari sauce, thyme, and hot sauce. Cook for 2 to 4 minutes until it has a thick consistency.
4. Transfer the cooked drumsticks to a plate. Top with the sauce and serve.

Crispy Chicken Tenders

Cooking Time: 25 minutes
Serves: 4

Ingredients:
- 1 pounds chicken tenders
- 2 tablespoons peanut oil
- 1 egg
- ½ cup tortilla chips, crushed
- ½ teaspoon garlic powder
- 1 teaspoon red pepper flakes
- Sea salt and ground black pepper, to taste
- 2 tablespoons peanuts, roasted and roughly chopped
- Cooking spray

Directions:
1. In a shallow bowl, beat egg. Fully mix the crushed chips, garlic powder, red pepper flakes, salt, and pepper in a separate bowl.
2. Rub the peanut oil all over the chicken tenders. Dredge the chicken tenders in the egg mixture, then in the chip mixture. Shake off the excess.
3. Spritz the air fryer basket with cooking spray. Arrange the tenders in the basket.
4. Put the air fryer lid on and cook in batches in the preheated instant pot at 350°F for 12 to 13 minutes until cooked through. Spritz the tenders with cooking spray and flip when the lid screen indicates 'TURN FOOD' halfway through the cooking time.
5. Remove the tenders from the basket to a plate and serve garnished with peanuts.

CHAPTER 5: FISH AND SEAFOOD RECIPES

Silky Cod with Snap Peas and Orange

Cooking Time: 30 minutes
Serves: 4

Ingredients:
- 4 (5-ounce) cod fillets
- 3 tablespoons butter, melted
- 2 tablespoons sesame seeds
- 3 cloves garlic, thinly sliced
- 2 packages (6-ounce) sugar snap peas
- 1 medium orange, cut into wedges
- Salt and ground black pepper to taste
- Cooking spray

Directions:
1. Rinse the cod fillets and dry thoroughly with paper towels on a plate, season with a touch of salt and pepper to taste. Set aside.
2. In a small bowl, mix the butter and sesame seeds, and stir well. Reserve 2 tablespoons of the mixture. Add the garlic and peas into the remaining butter mixture, then transfer to the air fryer basket. Spritz with cooking spray.
3. Put the air fryer lid on and cook in batches in the preheated instant pot at 400°F for 10 minutes. Stir the peas once halfway through the cooking, or until the peas are just tender. Remove the peas from the basket to a bowl.
4. Spread ½ of the remaining butter mixture on the both sides of the cod fillets to coat well. Lay the fillets in the air fryer basket. Put the air fryer lid on and cook for 4 minutes. Butter the fish fillets with remaining mixture and cook for an additional 6 minutes, or until the fish flesh is opaque.
5. Remove the fish fillets from the basket to a platter. Serve the fish fillets alongside the peas and orange wedges.

Breaded Fish Po' Boys with Chipotle Slaw

Cooking Time: 30 minutes
Serves: 4

Ingredients:
- 4 (4-ounce) fillets white fish, about ½- to 1-inch thick
- ¼ cup all-purpose flour
- ¼ teaspoon garlic powder
- ¼ teaspoon salt
- ½ teaspoon ground black pepper
- 1 egg, beaten
- 1 tablespoon water
- ½ cup panko bread crumbs
- ¼ cup cornmeal
- 4 hoagie rolls, split lengthwise and toasted
- 2 tablespoons crumbled queso fresco
- 4 lime wedges
- Cooking spray

Chipotle Slaw:
- ¼ cup mayonnaise
- ⅓ cup sour cream
- 1 tablespoon fresh lime juice
- ¼ teaspoon ground dried chipotle pepper
- ¼ teaspoon salt
- ¼ cup chopped fresh cilantro
- 3 cups cabbage with carrot, shredded (coleslaw mix)

Directions:
1. Rinse fish fillets under cold water, and dry thoroughly with paper towels. Set aside.
2. In a large bowl, mix together the flour, garlic powder, salt, and black pepper. In a small bowl, combine the egg and water. In a shallow dish, stir together the bread crumbs and cornmeal.
3. Dredge the fish fillets in the flour mixture, then into the egg mixture, and then into the bread crumb mixture.

4. Arrange the fish fillets in the air fryer basket, and spritz with cooking spray. Put the air fryer lid on and cook in batches in the preheated instant pot at 400°F for 6 to 10 minutes. Flip the fillets when the lid indicates 'TURN FOOD' halfway through the cooking.
5. To make the chipotle slaw, in a medium bowl, combine the mayo with sour cream, lime juice, dried chipotle pepper, and salt. Stir in the cilantro and coleslaw mix, and toss well.
6. To make the sandwiches, divide four fish fillets among half of each hoagie roll, and spread the chipotle slaw and queso fresco onto fish fillets, then finally top with the other half of hoagie rolls. Serve with lime wedges on the side.

Butter Tuna Zucchini

Cooking Time: 25 minutes
Serves: 4

Ingredients:
- 3 tablespoons butter, softened
- 1 (6-ounce) can chunk light tuna, drained
- 1 cup zucchini, shredded and drained by squeezing in a kitchen towel
- 4 corn tortillas
- 1 cup Cheddar or Colby cheese, shredded
- ⅓ cup mayonnaise
- 2 tablespoons mustard

Directions:
1. Brush the tortillas with the butter and arrange them in the air fryer basket.
2. Put the air fryer lid on and grill in the preheated instant pot at 350°F for 2 to 3 minutes until lightly browned.
3. Remove the tortillas from the basket to a plate. Set aside.
4. In a medium bowl, mix the tuna, zucchini, mayonnaise, and mustard. Toss to combine well.
5. Evenly divide the tuna mixture onto the tortillas and sprinkle the shredded cheese on top.
6. Transfer the tortillas into the basket and put the air fryer lid on. Cook for 2 to 4 minutes, or until the cheese melts.
7. Remove the tortillas from the basket to a serving dish. Serve warm.

Salmon Croquettes

Cooking Time: 20 minutes
Serves: 6

Ingredients:
- 1 can (14-ounce) salmon, drained and bones removed
- 1 egg, beaten
- ½ cup bread crumbs
- 2 scallions, diced
- 1 teaspoon garlic powder
- Salt and pepper to taste
- Cooking spray

Directions:
1. In a large bowl, mix together the beaten egg, bread crumbs, scallions and salmon. Season with garlic powder, salt and pepper. Toss to combine well.
2. To make the croquettes, scoop out the salmon mixture and shape into six equal-sized balls.
3. Arrange the croquettes in the air fryer basket and spritz with cooking spray.
4. Put the air fryer lid on and air fry in batches in the preheated instant pot at 375°F for 10 minutes. Flip the croquettes when it shows 'TURN FOOD' on the air fryer lid screen during cooking time, or until golden brown.
5. Transfer to a serving dish and cool for 5 minutes before serving.

Golden Beer-Battered Cod Fillets

Cooking Time: 35 minutes
Serves: 4

Ingredients:
- 1 cup malty beer
- (4-ounce) cod fillets
- 2 eggs
- 1 cup all-purpose flour
- ½ cup cornstarch
- 1 teaspoon garlic powder
- Salt and pepper to taste
- Cooking spray

Directions:
1. In a medium bowl, whisk together the egg and beer. In another bowl, mix the cornstarch and flour. Season with garlic, salt and pepper to taste. Stir to combine well.
2. Dredge the cod fillets in the cornstarch-flour mixture, then in the egg-beer mixture, and finally coat in the cornstarch-flour mixture again.
3. Spritz the air fryer basket with cooking spray. Arrange the coated cod fillets in the air fryer basket and spritz with cooking spray.
4. Put the air fryer lid on and cook in batches in the preheated instant pot at 375°F for 15 minutes. Flip the fillets when it shows 'TURN FOOD' on the air fryer lid screen during cooking time.
5. Transfer the fried fillets onto a serving plate. Cool for 3 minutes and serve alongside French fries, if desired.

Lemony Crab Cakes

Cooking Time: 15 minutes
Serves: 4

Ingredients:
- Juice of ½ lemon
- 8 ounces jumbo-sized lump crab meat
- 1 tablespoon Old Bay Seasoning
- ¼ cup red bell pepper, diced
- ¼ cup green bell pepper, diced
- 1 egg, beaten
- ¼ cup mayonnaise
- ⅓ cup bread crumbs
- 1 teaspoon flour
- Cooking spray

Directions:
1. In a large bowl, mix together the crab meat, Old Bay seasoning, bell peppers, egg, mayo, lemon juice, and bread crumbs. Toss well.
2. Scoop out the crab meat mixture and shape into 4 patties. Sprinkle each patty with ¼ teaspoon of flour.
3. Arrange the patties in the air fryer basket and spritz with cooking spray.
4. Put the air fryer lid on and cook in the preheated instant pot at 375°F for 10 minutes.
5. Transfer the crab patties (crab cakes) to a plate and enjoy.

Panko-Coated Coconut Shrimp

Cooking Time: 20 minutes
Serves: 4

Ingredients:
- 1 pound raw shrimp, peeled, deveined, rinsed, and drained
- ¼ cup panko bread crumbs
- 1 egg
- ¼ cup all-purpose flour
- ⅓ cup unsweetened coconut, shredded
- Salt and pepper to taste
- Cooking spray

Directions:
1. In a small bowl, whisk the egg until frothy. In another bowl, pour the flour. In a third bowl, mix together the coconut and bread crumbs, and season with salt and pepper.
2. Dredge the shrimp into the flour, then in the whisked egg, and then into the coconut-bread crumbs mixture to coat.
3. Spritz the air fryer basket with cooking spray. Arrange the shrimp in the basket and spray with cooking spray.
4. Put the air fryer lid on and cook in the preheated instant pot at 375°F for 8 minutes. Flip the shrimp when it shows 'TURN FOOD' on the lid screen during cooking time, or until the shrimps are opaque.
5. Transfer to a plate and cool for 3 minutes before serving.

Spiced Grilled Shrimp

Cooking Time: 15 minutes
Serves: 4

Ingredients:
- 1 pound raw shrimp, peeled and deveined
- 1 tablespoon paprika
- ½ tablespoon dried oregano
- ½ tablespoon cayenne pepper
- Juice of ½ lemon
- Salt and pepper to taste
- Cooking spray

Directions:
1. In a sealable plastic bag, put the shrimp, oregano, cayenne pepper, paprika, lemon juice, salt and pepper. Seal the bag and shake until the shrimp is coated thoroughly.
2. Transfer the coated shrimp to the air fryer basket and spray with cooking spray.
3. Put the air fryer lid on and cook in the preheated instant pot at 375°F for 8 minutes. Shake the basket when it shows 'TURN FOOD' on the air fryer lid screen during cooking time, or until the shrimp is cooked through.
4. Remove the shrimp from the basket to a plate. Allow to cool for 3 minutes and serve.

Wholesome Fennel Cod Meal

Cooking Time: 15 minutes
Serves: 2

Ingredients:
- ½ cup red pepper, thinly sliced
- ½ cup carrots, julienned
- 2 ½ ounces cod fillets, frozen and thawed
- ½ cup fennel bulbs, julienned
- 1 tablespoon lemon juice
- ½ teaspoon black pepper powder
- 2 tablespoons butter, melted
- 2 sprigs tarragon
- 1 tablespoon salt
- 1 tablespoon vegetable oil

Directions:
1. In a mixing bowl, combine the tarragon, melted butter, lemon juice, and ½ teaspoon salt. Mix the fennel bulbs, carrots and mix them well.
2. Coat the codfish fillets with the oil. Rub pepper and salt evenly.
3. Place the fillets over a baking sheet. Add the veggies on top. Use two baking sheets if needed.
4. Place Instant Pot Air Fryer Crisp over kitchen platform. Press Air Fry, set the temperature to 400°F and set the timer to 5 minutes to preheat. Press "Start" and allow it to pre-heat for 5 minutes.
5. In the inner pot, place the Air Fryer basket. In the basket, add the baking sheet with the fish.
6. Close the Crisp Lid and press the "Air Fry" setting. Set temperature to 350°F and set the timer to 15 minutes. Press "Start."
7. Halfway down, open the Crisp Lid, flip the fillets, and close the lid to continue cooking for the remaining time.
8. Open the Crisp Lid after cooking time is over. Serve warm.

Creamed Cod

Cooking Time: 10 minutes
Serves: 2

Ingredients:
- 1 tablespoon lemon juice
- ½ teaspoon ground black pepper
- ½ teaspoon salt
- 1 pound cod fillets
- 2 tablespoon olive oil
- Sauce:
- 3 tablespoons ground mustard
- 1 tablespoon butter
- ½ cup heavy cream
- ½ teaspoon salt

Directions:
1. Spread some olive oil on the fillets. Season with the salt, pepper, and lemon juice.
2. Grease Air Fryer Basket with some cooking spray. Place the fillets over.
3. Place Instant Pot Air Fryer Crisp over kitchen platform. Press Air Fry, set the temperature to 400°F and set the timer to 5 minutes to preheat. Press "Start" and allow it to pre-heat for 5 minutes.
4. In the inner pot, place the Air Fryer basket.
5. Close the Crisp Lid and press the "Air Fry" setting. Set temperature to 350°F and set the timer to 10 minutes. Press "Start."
6. Halfway down, open the Crisp Lid, flip the fillets, and close the lid to continue cooking for the remaining time.
7. Open the Crisp Lid after cooking time is over. Add the fish on a serving plate.
8. Press "Sauté," select "Hi" setting and press "Start." In the inner pot, add the heavy cream, mustard sauce, heavy cream, and salt. Cook for 3-4 minutes.
9. Pour it over the fish and serve warm.

Coconut Chili Shrimp

Cooking Time: 6 minutes   Serves: 5-6

Ingredients:
- 3 cups panko breadcrumbs
- ½ cup all-purpose flour
- 2 large eggs
- ½ teaspoon ground black pepper
- 2 teaspoon fresh cilantro, chopped
- 3 cups flaked coconut, unsweetened
- 12 ounce medium-size raw shrimps, peeled, and deveined)
- ¼ cup lime juice
- ¼ cup honey
- 1 serrano chili, thinly sliced
- ½ teaspoon kosher salt

Directions:
1. In a mixing bowl, combine honey, Serrano chili with lime juice.
2. In a mixing bowl, combine the pepper and flour. In a mixing bowl, beat the eggs.
3. In another bowl, combine the coconut and breadcrumbs. Coat the shrimps with the eggs, then with the flour, and then with the crumbs. Coat with some cooking spray.
4. Place Instant Pot Air Fryer Crisp over kitchen platform. Press Air Fry, set the temperature to 400°F and set the timer to 5 minutes to preheat. Press "Start" and allow it to pre-heat for 5 minutes.
5. In the inner pot, place the Air Fryer basket. Line with a parchment paper, add the shrimps.
6. Close the Crisp Lid and press the "Air Fry" setting. Set temperature to 200°F and set the timer to 6 minutes. Press "Start."
7. Halfway down, open the Crisp Lid, shake the basket and close the lid to continue cooking for the remaining time.
8. Open the Crisp Lid after cooking time is over. Serve the shrimps warm with the chili sauce.
9. Nutrition:
10. Calories: 233 Fat: 8.5g Saturated Fat: 1g Trans Fat: 0g Carbohydrates: 28g Fiber: 6g Sodium: 349mg Protein: 13g

Mustard Salmon

Cooking Time: 10 minutes
Serves: 2

Ingredients:
- ½ teaspoon ground black pepper
- 2 tablespoons mustard, whole grain
- 1 garlic clove, grated
- 2 salmon fillets
- 2 teaspoon virgin olive oil
- 1 tablespoon brown sugar
- ½ teaspoon thyme leaves

Directions:
1. Rub the salmon with pepper and salt. In a mixing bowl, combine the mustard grain, thyme, garlic, brown sugar, and olive oil. Coat the salmon with the mixture.
2. Place Instant Pot Air Fryer Crisp over kitchen platform. Press Air Fry, set the temperature to 400°F and set the timer to 5 minutes to preheat. Press "Start" and allow it to pre-heat for 5 minutes.
3. In the inner pot, place the Air Fryer basket. In the basket, add the salmon.
4. Close the Crisp Lid and press the "Air Fry" setting. Set temperature to 400°F and set the timer to 10 minutes. Press "Start."
5. Halfway down, open the Crisp Lid, flip the salmon, and close the lid to continue cooking for the remaining time.
6. Open the Crisp Lid after cooking time is over. Serve warm.

Bacon Shrimps

Cooking Time: 10 minutes
Serves: 5-6

Ingredients:
- 1/2 teaspoon cayenne pepper
- 1/2 teaspoon ground cumin
- 1/2 teaspoon onion powder
- 1 pound shrimp
- 1 package bacon
- 1 teaspoon garlic powder
- 1/2 teaspoon lemon zest
- 1 tablespoon lemon juice
- 1 tablespoon Worcestershire sauce

Directions:
1. In a mixing bowl, whisk the Worcestershire sauce, cayenne pepper, onion powder, cumin, lemon zest, and garlic powder. Add and combine the shrimp. Refrigerate for 1-2 hours to marinate.
2. Take the bacon, slice into two parts, and wrap each shrimp with them.
3. Place Instant Pot Air Fryer Crisp over kitchen platform. Press Air Fry, set the temperature to 400°F and set the timer to 5 minutes to preheat. Press "Start" and allow it to pre-heat for 5 minutes.
4. In the inner pot, place the Air Fryer basket. In the basket, add the wrapped shrimps.
5. Close the Crisp Lid and press the "Air Fry" setting. Set temperature to 380°F and set the timer to 10 minutes. Press "Start."
6. Halfway down, open the Crisp Lid, shake the basket and close the lid to continue cooking for the remaining time.
7. Open the Crisp Lid after cooking time is over. Serve warm.

Cajuned Salmon Meal

Cooking Time: 8 minutes
Serves: 2

Ingredients:
- 1 tablespoon Cajun seasoning
- 2 salmon fillets (6 ounce each and with skin)
- 1 teaspoon brown sugar

Directions:
1. In a mixing bowl, combine Cajun seasoning and brown sugar. Add the fillets and coat well.
2. Place Instant Pot Air Fryer Crisp over kitchen platform. Press Air Fry, set the temperature to 400°F and set the timer to 5 minutes to preheat. Press "Start" and allow it to pre-heat for 5 minutes.
3. In the inner pot, place the Air Fryer basket. Spray it with some cooking oil, and in the basket, add the fillets.
4. Close the Crisp Lid and press the "Air Fry" setting. Set temperature to 390°F and set the timer to 8 minutes. Press "Start."
5. Halfway down, open the Crisp Lid, flip the fillets, and close the lid to continue cooking for the remaining time.
6. Open the Crisp Lid after cooking time is over. Serve warm.

Garlic Lemon Shrimp

Cooking Time: 5 minutes
Serves: 4

Ingredients:
- ¼ teaspoon, crushed red pepper flakes
- 1 tablespoon virgin olive oil
- 1 pound small shrimps, peeled and deveined
- 1 lemon juice, zested
- ¼ cup, parsley, chopped
- 4 cloves garlic, finely grated
- ¼ teaspoon salt

Directions:
1. Remove the tails of the shrimps. In a mixing bowl, add the garlic, lemon zest, shrimps, red pepper flakes, salt, and olive oil. Combine the ingredients to mix well with each other.
2. Place Instant Pot Air Fryer Crisp over kitchen platform. Press Air Fry, set the temperature to 400°F and set the timer to 5 minutes to preheat. Press "Start" and allow it to pre-heat for 5 minutes.
3. In the inner pot, place the Air Fryer basket. In the basket, add the shrimps.
4. Close the Crisp Lid and press the "Air Fry" setting. Set temperature to 400°F and set the timer to 6 minutes. Press "Start."
5. Halfway down, open the Crisp Lid, shake the basket and close the lid to continue cooking for the remaining time.
6. Open the Crisp Lid after cooking time is over. Serve warm with the lemon juice and parsley on top.

CHAPTER 6: VEGETABLES AND VEGAN RECIPES

Cauliflower Bites

Cooking Time: 16 minutes
Serves: 4

Ingredients:
- Cauliflower head – 1, cut into florets
- Old bay seasoning – ½ tsp.
- Paprika – ¼ tsp.
- Garlic – 1 tbsp., minced
- Olive oil – 3 tbsps.
- Pepper & salt, to taste

Directions:
1. Add cauliflower florets into the large bowl. Add remaining ingredients and toss well. Add cauliflower florets into the multi-level air fryer basket and place basket into the instant pot. Seal pot with the air fryer lid. Select air fry mode and cook at 400 F for 16 minutes. Turn cauliflower florets halfway through. Serve.

Healthy Broccoli Bites

Cooking Time: 5 minutes
Serves: 2

Ingredients:
- Broccoli florets – 4 cups
- Olive oil – 2 tbsps.
- Nutritional yeast – 1 tbsp.
- Pepper & salt, to taste

Directions:
1. Add broccoli florets and remaining ingredients into the mixing bowl and toss well. Add broccoli florets into the multi-level air fryer basket and place basket into the instant pot. Seal pot with the air fryer lid. Select air fry mode and cook at 370 F for 5 minutes. Serve.

Asparagus with Almonds

Cooking Time: 5 minutes
Serves: 4

Ingredients:
- Asparagus spears – 16, trimmed
- Olive oil – 2 tbsps.
- Balsamic vinegar – 2 tbsps.
- Sliced almonds – 1/3 cup
- Pepper & salt, to taste

Directions:
1. In a bowl, toss asparagus with oil and balsamic vinegar. Add asparagus spears into the multi-level air fryer basket. Sprinkle sliced almonds on top of asparagus. Place the basket into the instant pot. Seal pot with air fryer lid. Select air fry mode and cook at 350 F for 5 minutes. Serve.

Sesame Carrots

Cooking Time: 14 minutes   Serves: 4

Ingredients:
- Sliced carrots – 2 cups
- Sesame seeds – 1 tsp.
- Green onion – 1 tbsp.
- Garlic – 1 tsp., minced
- Soy sauce – 1 tbsp.
- Ginger – 1 tbsp., minced
- Sesame oil – 2 tbsps.

Directions:
1. In a mixing bowl, add all ingredients, except green onion and sesame seeds. Pour carrot mixture into the multi-level air fryer basket and place the basket into the instant pot. Seal pot with the air fryer lid. Select air fry mode and cook at 375 F for 14 minutes. Stir halfway through. Garnish with green onion and sesame seeds. Serve.

Perfect Zucchini & Squash

Cooking Time: 20 minutes
Serves: 4

Ingredients:
- Zucchini – 1 pound, cut into ½-inch half-moons
- Yellow squash – 1 pound, cut into ½-inch half-moons
- Olive oil – 2 tsps.
- Pepper & salt, to taste

Directions:
1. Add zucchini and squash into the mixing bowl. Add oil, pepper, and salt and toss well. Transfer zucchini and squash into the multi-level air fryer basket and place basket into the instant pot. Seal pot with the air fryer lid. Select air fry mode and cook at 400 F for 20 minutes. Stir halfway through. Serve.

Roasted Carrots

Cooking Time: 20 minutes
Serves: 2

Ingredients:
- Baby carrots – 8 oz
- Olive oil – 1 tbsp.
- Brown sugar – 1 tbsp.
- Pepper & salt, to taste

Directions:
1. In a mixing bowl, toss baby carrots with remaining ingredients. Add baby carrots into the multi-level air fryer basket and place basket into the instant pot. Seal pot with the air fryer lid. Select air fry mode and cook at 360 F for 20 minutes. Stir halfway through. Serve.

Healthy Brussels Sprouts & Sweet Potatoes

Cooking Time: 16 minutes   Serves: 6

Ingredients:
- Brussels sprouts – 1 pound, cut in half
- Sweet potatoes – 1 pound, cut into ½-inch cubes
- Black pepper – ½ tsp.
- Chili powder – 1 tsp.
- Olive oil – 4 tbsps.
- Pepper & salt, to taste

Directions:
1. Add sweet potatoes and Brussels sprouts into the mixing bowl. Add remaining ingredients and toss well. Transfer sweet potatoes and Brussels sprouts mixture into the multi-level air fryer basket and place the basket into the instant pot. Seal pot with the air fryer lid. Select air fry mode and cook at 380 F for 16 minutes. Stir halfway through. Serve.

Parmesan Brussels Sprouts

Cooking Time: 12 minutes   Serves: 4

Ingredients:
- Brussels sprouts – 2 cups, cut in half
- Bagel seasoning – 2 tbsps.
- Sliced almonds – 4 tbsps.
- Grated parmesan cheese – 4 tbsps.
- Olive oil – 2 tbsps.
- Pepper & salt, to taste

Directions:
1. Add 2 cups of water and Brussels sprouts into the saucepan and cook over medium heat for 10 minutes. Drain Brussels sprouts well and place in a mixing bowl. Add the remaining ingredients over the Brussels sprouts and toss well. Transfer Brussels sprouts mixture into the multi-level air fryer basket and place basket into the instant pot. Seal pot with air fryer lid. Select air fry mode and cook at 375 F for 12 minutes. Stir halfway through. Serve.

Flavorful Cauliflower

Cooking Time: 20 minutes
Serves: 4

Ingredients:
- Cauliflower florets – 4 cups
- Ground cumin – 1 tsp.
- Olive oil – 2 tbsps.
- Garlic cloves – 2, minced
- Pepper & salt, to taste

Directions:
1. Toss cauliflower florets with remaining ingredients into the bowl. Transfer cauliflower florets into the multi-level air fryer basket and place basket into the instant pot. Seal pot with the air fryer lid. Select air fry mode and cook at 400 F for 20 minutes. Stir halfway through. Serve.

Quick & Easy Green Beans

Cooking Time: 10 minutes
Serves: 2

Ingredients:
- Green beans – 2 cups
- Olive oil – 2 tbsps.
- Shawarma spice mix – 1 tbsp.
- Pepper & salt, to taste

Directions:
1. Toss green beans with shawarma spice, oil, and salt. Place green beans into the multi-level air fryer basket and place the basket into the instant pot. Seal pot with the air fryer lid. Select air fry mode and cook at 370 F for 10 minutes. Turn green beans halfway through. Serve.

Rosemary air-fried potatoes

Cooking time: 15 minutes
Serves: 4

Ingredients:
- 3 tbsp. Vegetable oil
- 4 yellow baby potatoes (quartered
- 2 tsp. Dried rosemary minced
- 1 tbsp. Minced garlic
- 1 tsp. Ground black pepper
- 1/4 cup chopped parsley
- 1 tbsp. Fresh lime or lemon juice
- 1 tsp. Salt

Directions:
1. Add potatoes, garlic, rosemary, pepper, and salt in a large bowl. Mix thoroughly.
2. Arrange seasoned potatoes in the air fryer basket and place it inside the instant pot duo. Cover with the air fryer lid and air fry at 400 degrees Fahrenheit for about 15 minutes.
3. Check to see if tomatoes are cooked through since it depends on the size of potatoes.
4. Once cooked, take it out of the air fryer and place in a platter.
5. Sprinkle with lemon juice and parsley.
6. Serve warm.

Air Fryer Falafel Balls

Cooking time: 12 minutes   Serves: 3

Ingredients:
- ½ cup sweet onion (diced
- 2 tbsp. Olive oil
- ½ tsp. Turmeric
- ½ cup carrots (minced
- 1 cup rolled oats
- ½ cup roasted - salted cashews
- 2 cups cooked chickpeas (drained and rinsed
- Juice of 1 fresh lemon
- 2 tbsp. Soy sauce
- 1 tbsp. Flax meal
- ½ tsp. Garlic powder
- ½ tsp. Ground cumin

Directions:
1. Put a little olive oil and sauté onions and carrots in the instant pot duo. Cook for about 7 minutes and transfer onions and carrots to a large bowl. Use the pressure cooker lid and do not forget to detach it after using.
2. Place cashew and oats in a food processor and process until you achieve a coarse meal consistency. Add the mixture to the bowl with the vegetables.
3. Next, place chickpeas with the lemon juice and soy sauce into the food processor, puree until semi-smooth in consistency.
4. Transfer it to the bowl and add in the flax and spices. Stir to blend. Make sure that everything is well mixed.
5. Using your hands, form falafel balls from the dough and arrange them single layer in the air fryer basket lined with parchment paper. You may use two layered air fryer to accommodate all in a single batch. Place the air fryer basket into the instant pot and attach the air fryer lid to cover. Secure lock and air fry at 370 degrees Fahrenheit for 12 minutes. Shake the basket after 8 minutes for even cooking,
6. Serve dish on top of salad greens with magical tahini dressing.

Air Fried Cauliflower Rice

Cooking time: 15 minutes   Serves: 2

Ingredients:
- Cups cauliflower florets
- 3 cloves of garlic
- 1/2 tsp. Smoked paprika
- 1 tbsp. Peanut oil

Directions:
1. Smash garlic using the blade of a knife.
2. Place all ingredients in a mixing bowl and mix to coat cauliflower florets with the seasoning.
3. Line the air fryer basket with parchment paper and place coated florets in it.
4. Insert the basket inside instant pot air fryer crisp and attach the air fryer lid.
5. Air fry for 15 minutes at 400 degrees Fahrenheit, shaking the air fryer basket every 5 minutes. If you want it crispier, cook for an additional 5 minutes.
6. Serve and enjoy!

Seasoned Zucchini & Squash

Cooking time: 10 minutes   Serves: 6

Ingredients:
- 2 large yellow squash, cut into slices
- 2 large zucchinis, cut into slices
- ¼ cup olive oil
- ½ onion, sliced
- ¾ teaspoon Italian seasoning
- ½ teaspoon garlic salt
- ¼ teaspoon seasoned salt

Directions:
1. In a large bowl, mix together all the ingredients.
2. Press "power button" of air fry oven and turn the dial to select the "air fry" mode.
3. Press the time button and again turn the dial to set the cooking time to 10 minutes.
4. Now push the temp button and rotate the dial to set the temperature at 400 degrees f.
5. Press "start/pause" button to start.
6. When the unit beeps to show that it is preheated, open the lid.
7. Arrange the squash mixture in "air fry basket" and insert in the oven.
8. Serve hot.

Garlicky Brussels Sprout

Cooking time: 12 minutes
Serves: 4

Ingredients:
- 1 lb. Brussels sprouts, cut in half
- 2 tablespoons oil
- 2 garlic cloves, minced
- ¼ teaspoon red pepper flakes, crushed
- Salt and ground black pepper, as required

Directions:
1. In a bowl, add all the ingredients and toss to coat well.
2. Press "power button" of air fry oven and turn the dial to select the "air fry" mode.
3. Press the time button and again turn the dial to set the cooking time to 12 minutes.
4. Now push the temp button and rotate the dial to set the temperature at 390 degrees f.
5. Press "start/pause" button to start.
6. When the unit beeps to show that it is preheated, open the lid.
7. Arrange the brussels sprouts in "air fry basket" and insert in the oven.
8. Serve hot.

Sweet & Sour Brussels Sprout

Cooking time: 10 minutes
Serves: 2

Ingredients:
- 2 cups brussels sprouts, trimmed and halved lengthwise
- 1 tablespoon balsamic vinegar
- 1 tablespoon maple syrup
- ¼ teaspoon red pepper flakes, crushed
- Salt, as required

Directions:
1. In a bowl, add all the ingredients and toss to coat well.
2. Press "power button" of air fry oven and turn the dial to select the "air fry" mode.
3. Press the time button and again turn the dial to set the cooking time to 10 minutes.
4. Now push the temp button and rotate the dial to set the temperature at 400 degrees f.
5. Press "start/pause" button to start.
6. When the unit beeps to show that it is preheated, open the lid.
7. Arrange the brussels sprouts in "air fry basket" and insert in the oven.
8. Serve hot.

CHAPTER 7: DESSERTS RECIPES

Brownie Muffins

Cooking Time: 15 minutes
Serves: 6

Ingredients:
- Cocoa powder – 1/4 cup
- Almond butter – 1/2 cup
- Pumpkin puree – 1 cup
- Liquid stevia – 8 drops
- Protein powder – 2 scoops

Directions:
1. Add all ingredients into the mixing bowl and beat until smooth. Pour batter into the 6 silicone muffin moulds. Place the dehydrating tray into the multi-level air fryer basket and place the basket into the instant pot. Place muffin moulds on a dehydrating tray. Seal pot with the air fryer lid. Select bake mode and cook at 350 F for 15 minutes. Serve.

Delicious Lemon Muffins

Cooking Time: 15 minutes
Serves: 6

Ingredients:
- Egg – 1
- Baking powder – 3/4 tsp.
- Lemon zest – 1 tsp., grated
- Sugar – 1/2 cup
- Vanilla – 1/2 tsp.
- Milk – 1/2 cup
- Canola oil – 2 tbsps.
- Baking soda – 1/4 tsp.
- Flour – 1 cup
- Salt – 1/2 tsp.

Directions:
1. In a mixing bowl, beat egg, vanilla, milk, oil, and sugar until creamy. Add remaining ingredients and stir to combine. Pour batter into the 6 silicone muffin moulds. Place the dehydrating tray into the multi-level air fryer basket and place the basket into the instant pot. Place muffin moulds on a dehydrating tray. Seal pot with the air fryer lid. Select bake mode and cook at 350 F for 15 minutes. Serve.

Vanilla Strawberry Soufflé

Cooking Time: 15 minutes
Serves: 4

Ingredients:
- Egg whites – 3
- Strawberries – 1 1/2 cups.
- Vanilla – 1/2 tsp.
- Sugar – 1 tbsp.

Directions:
1. Spray 4 ramekins with cooking spray and set aside. Add strawberries, sugar, and vanilla into the blender and blend until smooth. Add egg whites into the bowl and beat until medium peaks form. Add strawberry mixture and fold well. Pour egg mixture into the ramekins. Place the dehydrating tray into the multi-level air fryer basket and place the basket into the instant pot. Place ramekins on the dehydrating tray. Seal pot with the air fryer lid. Select bake mode and cook at 350 F for 15 minutes. Serve.

Healthy Carrot Muffins

Cooking Time: 20 minutes
Serves: 6

Ingredients:
- Egg – 1
- Vanilla – 1 tsp.
- Brown sugar – 1/4 cup
- Granulated sugar – 1/4 cup
- Canola oil – 1/2 tbsp.
- Applesauce – 1/4 cup
- All-purpose flour – 1 cup
- Baking powder – 1 1/2 tsps.
- Nutmeg – 1/4 tsp.
- Cinnamon – 1 tsp.
- Grated carrots – 3/4 cup
- Salt – 1/4 tsp.

Directions:
1. Add all ingredients into a large bowl and mix until thoroughly combined. Pour batter into 6 silicone muffin moulds. Place the dehydrating tray into the multi-level air fryer basket and place the basket into the instant pot. Place muffin molds on the dehydrating tray. Seal pot with the air fryer lid. Select bake mode and cook at 350 F for 20 minutes. Serve.

Cinnamon Carrot Cake

Cooking Time: 25 minutes
Serves: 4

Ingredients:
- Egg – 1
- Vanilla – 1/2 tsp.
- Cinnamon – 1/2 tsp.
- Sugar – 1/2 cup
- Canola oil – 1/4 cup
- Walnuts – 1/4, chopped
- Baking powder – 1/2 tsp.
- Flour – 1/2 cup
- Grated carrot – 1/4 cup

Directions:
1. Spray a baking dish with cooking spray and set aside. In a mixing bowl, beat sugar and oil for 1-2 minutes. Add vanilla, cinnamon, and egg and beat for 30 seconds. Add remaining ingredients and stir to combine. Pour batter into the prepared baking dish. Place steam rack into the instant pot. Place baking dish on top of the steam rack. Seal pot with the air fryer lid. Select bake mode and cook at 350 F for 25 minutes. Serve.

Air Fryer Doughnuts

Cooking time: 1 hour & 40 minutes
Serves: 6

Ingredients:
- 2 cup all-purpose flour
- ½ cup milk
- ¼ cup + 1 teaspoon granulated sugar
- 2¼ teaspoon active-dry east
- 4 tablespoons melted butter
- 1 egg, large
- 1 teaspoon vanilla essence
- ½ teaspoon kosher salt
- Vegetable oil, cooking spray
- For the Vanilla Glaze:
- ½ teaspoon vanilla extract
- 2 ounces milk
- 1 cup of sugar powder
- For the Chocolate Glaze:
- ¼ cup cocoa powder, unsweetened
- ¾ cup of sugar powder
- 3 tablespoons milk
- For the Cinnamon Sugar:
- 2 tablespoons ground cinnamon
- ½ cup granulated sugar
- 2 tablespoons melted butter

Directions:
1. For making the Doughnuts:
2. Microwave the milk for 40 seconds in an oven-safe glass bowl.
3. Add sugar and stir until it dissolves.
4. After that, drizzle some yeast and keep it aside to froth. Within 8-10 minutes, it will froth.
5. Combine salt and flour in a medium bowl.
6. Spray some cooking oil in a large bowl and combine butter, ¼ sugar, vanilla,

and egg.

7. Transfer the yeast mixture into it and combine it thoroughly.
8. After that add, the dry mixture kept ready in the medium bowl. Combine the mix to become a rough dough.
9. Drizzle some flour on your kitchen working table and transfer the dough onto it.
10. Knead it gently for 5 minutes until it becomes soft and change to elastic texture.
11. Maintain the consistency of the dough by adding the flour.
12. Shape the dough into a ball and transfer into a greased bowl.
13. Cover it with a dish towel and keep it in a warm place for 1 hour to raise the dough to its double size.
14. Take a baking tray and line with a parchment paper.
15. Spritz cooking oil and place the dough on it.
16. Place the dough on a floured working table and spread the dough, pressing with your palm and make it into a ½" thick flat sheet.
17. Using a 3" diameter doughnut cutter, make doughnuts with holes.
18. Transfer the doughnuts into the parchment paper.
19. You can use the remaining doughs and knead it make fresh doughnuts.
20. Place the baking tray in the air fryer basket and place the air fryer basket into the inner pot of the Instant Pot Air Fryer.
21. Close the crisp cover and set the temperature to 375°F in the BAKE mode.
22. Set the timer to 6 minutes.
23. Press START to begin baking and continue cooking until it becomes golden brown.
24. For making the vanilla glaze, whisk milk, vanilla, and sugar powder in a medium bowl until it turns smooth. Dip the doughnuts in the glaze.
25. For making the chocolate glaze, combine cocoa powder, milk, and powdered sugar in a medium bowl, until it becomes soft. Dip the doughnuts in the glaze.
26. For making the cinnamon sugar, whisk sugar, and ground cinnamon in a large shallow bowl. Apply butter on the doughnuts and sprinkle the cinnamon sugar on it.
27. After glazing and sugaring, allow the doughnuts to settle down the heat before you serve.

Air Fryer Cinnamon Rolls

Cooking time: 25 minutes
Serves: 6

Ingredients:
- For the Rolls:
- 8 ounces Crescent rolls, refrigerated
- 2 tablespoons butter melted.
- ⅓ cup brown sugar
- ½ teaspoon ground cinnamon
- ½ teaspoon kosher salt
- 4 tablespoons flour for kneading support
- For the Glaze:
- ½ cup of sugar powder
- 1 tablespoon whole milk
- 2 ounces cream cheese, kept in room temperature

Directions:
1. Whisk brown sugar and ground cinnamon and the required amount of salt.
2. Flour your working table and spread out the crescent roll.
3. Apply butter lavishly on the crescent roll sheet.
4. Sprinkle the sugar-cinnamon mixture on the buttered area.
5. Roll it up and crimp the edge.
6. Cut the roll into 3 pieces.
7. Repeat all the rolls like this.
8. Place the cinnamon rolls in the air fryer basket.
9. Put the air fryer basket in the inner pot of the Instant Pot Air Fryer.
10. Close the crisp cover.
11. Select the temperature to 350°F and set the timer to 10 minutes in the BAKE mode.
12. Do not over crowed the basket. If required, you can bake in batches.
13. Press START to begin baking.
14. For making the glaze, whisk milk, cream cheese, and sugar powder in a medium bowl until it becomes smooth.
15. After baking, remove it from the Air Fryer.
16. Now spread the glaze on top of the cinnamon rolls and serve.

Air Fryer Molten Lava Cake

Cooking time: 10 minutes
Serves: 4

Ingredients:
- 3½ ounces dark chocolates
- 2 eggs
- 3½ tablespoons baker's sugar, granules
- 1½ tablespoon self-rising flour
- 2 tablespoons butter melted
- 4 ramekins of standard size

Directions:
1. In the AIR FRY mode, set your Instant Pot Air Fryer at 375°F and timer for 5 minutes for preheating.
2. Press START to begin preheating.
3. Grease the ramekins with melted butter.
4. Microwave the dark chocolate in an oven-safe glass bowl at high intensity for 2 minutes, until it starts to melt.
5. When the chocolates melted completely, remove it from the microwave oven and stir to maintain its consistency.
6. Beat the eggs in a medium bowl until it becomes frothy.
7. Transfer the melted chocolate into the beaten egg.
8. Add self-rising flour and combine thoroughly.
9. Fill three forth portion of the ramekins.
10. Put in the air fryer basket and place in the inner pot of the Instant Pot Air fryer.
11. Close the crisp cover.
12. In BAKE Mode, set the temperature at 375°F and the timer to 10 minutes.
13. Press START to resume baking.
14. After 10 minutes, remove it from the air fryer and allow it to settle down the heat for 2-3 minutes.
15. Flip down the ramekin to the serving place and tap on the bottom side to force it to fall.

Crustless Cheesecake in Instant Pot Air Fryer

Cooking time: 10 minutes
Serves: 4

Ingredients:
- 16 ounces cream cheese, kept in room temperature
- 2 eggs
- ¾ cup sweetener, low calorie
- ½ teaspoon lemon zest
- 1 teaspoon vanilla extract
- 2 tablespoons sour cream

Directions:
1. In AIR FRY mode, set the temperature of Instant Pot Air Fryer to 350°F and timer to 5 minutes for preheating. Press START to begin preheating.
2. Combine eggs, vanilla, lemon juice, and sweetener in a blender until it becomes smooth.
3. Add cream cheese, sour cream, and continue blending until it becomes soft cream and lump-free.
4. Transfer the cream into a 4-inch springform pan.
5. Put in the air fryer basket and place in the inner pot of the Instant Pot Air Fryer.
6. Close the crisp lid.
7. In the BAKE mode keeping the temperature at 350°F, select the timer for 10 minutes.
8. Press START to begin baking.
9. After cooking, remove it from the air fryer and allow it to cool down.
10. Refrigerate for 3 hours before you want to serve.

Air Fryer Chocolate Chip Cookie

Cooking time: 10 minutes   Serves: 8

Ingredients:
- 1 cup chocolate chunks
- 1½ cup all-purpose flour
- ½ cup butter kept in room temperature
- ½ cup of sugar
- ½ cup brown sugar
- ½ teaspoon baking soda
- 1 egg
- 1 teaspoon vanilla extract
- ¼ teaspoon kosher salt

Directions:
1. Let us preheat the Instant Pot Air Fryer.
2. In the AIR FRY mode, set the temperature to 350°F and timer for 5 minutes.
3. Press START to begin preheating.
4. Take two baking pans that can accommodate in the air fryer and grease it.
5. In a medium bowl, combine sugar, butter, and brown sugar.
6. Add vanilla, egg, and whisk thoroughly.
7. Stir in salt, flour, and baking soda.
8. Finally, add chocolate chunks and combine them thoroughly.
9. Transfer half of the cookie dough into one baking pan. The remaining portion you can transfer into the other baking pan.
10. Press the cookie dough firmly to the bottom of the pan.
11. Put the pan in the air fryer basket and place the air fryer basket in the inner pot of the Instant Pot Air Fryer.
12. Close the crisp lid.
13. In the BAKE mode, select temperature at 350°F, and timer to 12 minutes.
14. Press START to begin baking and continue baking until it turns slightly brown.
15. Once it is ready, allow it to cool down for 4-5 minutes.
16. Slice and serve.

Cherry-Choco Bars

Cooking Time: 15 minutes
Serves: 8

Ingredients:
- ¼ teaspoon salt
- ½ cup almonds, sliced
- ½ cup chia seeds
- ½ cup dark chocolate, chopped
- ½ cup dried cherries, chopped
- ½ cup prunes, pureed
- ½ cup quinoa, cooked
- ¾ cup almond butter
- 1/3 cup honey
- 2 cups old-fashioned oats
- 2 tablespoon coconut oil

Directions:
1. Preparing the Ingredients. Preheat the Instant Crisp Air Fryer to 375°F.
2. In a mixing bowl, combine the oats, quinoa, chia seeds, almond, cherries, and chocolate.
3. In a saucepan, heat the almond butter, honey, and coconut oil.
4. Pour the butter mixture over the dry mixture. Add salt and prunes. Mix until well combined.
5. Pour over a baking dish that can fit inside the Instant Crisp Air Fryer.
6. Air Frying. Close the air fryer Lid. Select Bake, Cook for 15 minutes at 375°F.
7. Let it cool for an hour before slicing into bars.

CHAPTER 8: APPETIZERS AND SNACKS

Zucchini Crisps

Cooking Time: 12 minutes
Serves: 2

Ingredients:
- Medium zucchini – 1, sliced 1/4–inch thick
- Parmesan cheese – ½ cup, grated
- Olive oil – 1 tbsp.

Directions:
1. Brush zucchini slices with oil and coat with parmesan cheese. Place zucchini slices into the multi-level air fryer basket and place basket into the instant pot. Seal pot with air fryer lid. Select air fry mode and cook at 370 F for 12 minutes. Serve.

Delicious Chickpeas

Cooking Time: 17 minutes
Serves: 4

Ingredients:
- Can chickpeas – 15 oz, drained
- For seasoning:
- Black pepper – ½ tsp.
- Dry mustard – ½ tsp.
- Garlic powder – ½ tsp.
- Brown sugar – 1 tsp.
- Paprika – 1 ½ tsp.
- Salt – ½ tsp

Directions:
1. Spread chickpeas in the multi-level air fryer basket and place basket into the instant pot. Seal pot with the air fryer lid. Select air fry mode and cook at 390 F for 17 minutes. Stir halfway through. Once done, then transfer chickpeas into the mixing bowl. Add all seasoning ingredients and toss until well coated. Serve.

Crispy Green Beans

Cooking Time: 5 minutes
Serves: 2

Ingredients:
- Green beans – ½ pound, wash & trimmed
- Egg– 1, lightly beaten
- Garlic powder – ¼ tsp.
- Onion powder – 1/4 tsp.
- Parmesan cheese – 2 tbsps., grated
- Breadcrumbs – ½ cup
- Pepper & salt, to taste

Directions:
1. In a shallow bowl, add the egg. In a separate shallow dish, mix together breadcrumbs, cheese, onion powder, garlic powder, pepper, and salt. Dip green beans in egg and coat with breadcrumb mixture. Place coated green beans into the multi-level air fryer basket and place basket into the instant pot. Seal pot with the air fryer lid. Select air fry mode and cook at 390 F for 5 minutes. Serve.

Garlicky Almonds

Cooking Time: 6 minutes   Serves: 4

Ingredients:
- Almonds – 1 cup
- Black pepper – 1/8 tsp.
- Paprika – ½ tsp.
- Garlic powder – ½ tbsp.
- Soy sauce – ½ tbsp.

Directions:
1. In a bowl, mix together black pepper, paprika, garlic powder, and soy sauce. Add almonds and coat well. Transfer almonds into the multi-level air fryer basket and place basket into the instant pot. Seal pot with the air fryer lid. Select air fry mode and cook at 320 F for 6 minutes. Stir halfway through. Serve.

Eggplant Chips

Cooking Time: 30 minutes
Serves: 2

Ingredients:
- Eggplant – 1, sliced ¼-inch thick
- Fresh rosemary – 2 tbsps., chopped
- Olive oil – 1 tbsp.
- Parmesan cheese – ½ cup, grated
- Pepper & salt, to taste

Directions:
1. Toss eggplant slices in a mixing bowl with rosemary, oil, parmesan cheese, pepper, and salt. Place eggplant slices into the multi-level air fryer basket and place basket into the instant pot. Seal pot with the air fryer lid. Select air fry mode and cook at 400 F for 30 minutes. Turn eggplant slices halfway through. Serve.

Air Fried Simple Tofu Bites

Cooking Time: 20 minutes
Serves: 4

Ingredients:
- 10 oz tofu, cut into cubes
- 1 1/2 tbsp dried rosemary
- 1 tsp vinegar
- 2 tsp olive oil
- Pepper
- Salt

Directions:
1. Add tofu and remaining ingredients into the large bowl and toss well.
2. Spray instant pot multi-level air fryer basket with cooking spray.
3. Add tofu cubes into the air fryer basket and place basket into the instant pot.
4. Seal pot with air fryer lid and select air fry mode then set the temperature to 350 F and timer for 20 minutes. Stir halfway through.
5. Serve and enjoy.

Salmon Crisps

Cooking Time: 12 minutes
Serves: 2-4

Ingredients:
- 2 tablespoons dill, chopped
- ½ cup panko breadcrumbs
- ¼ teaspoon ground black pepper
- 2 teaspoons mustard, Dijon
- 2 tablespoons of canola mayonnaise
- 2 cans (7.5 ounces) salmon, unsalted, with bones and skin
- 2 lemon wedges
- 1 egg, large

Directions:
1. In a mixing bowl, add the salmon, dill, panko, mayonnaise, pepper, and mustard. Combine the ingredients to mix well with each other. Prepare cakes from the mixture.
2. Grease Air Fryer Basket with some cooking spray.
3. Place Instant Pot Air Fryer Crisp over kitchen platform. Press Air Fry, set the temperature to 400°F and set the timer to 5 minutes to preheat. Press "Start" and allow it to preheat for 5 minutes.
4. In the inner pot, place the Air Fryer basket. In the basket, add the salmon cakes.
5. Close the Crisp Lid and press the "Bake" setting. Set temperature to 400°F and set the timer to 12 minutes. Press "Start." Flip the cakes halfway down.
6. Open the Crisp Lid after cooking time is over. Serve with your choice of dip or tomato ketchup.

Wholesome Asparagus

Cooking Time: 10 minutes
Serves: 4

Ingredients:
- 1-pound (½ bunch) asparagus, washed and trimmed
- ½ teaspoon Himalayan salt
- 1 olive oil spray
- 1/4 teaspoon garlic powder
- 1 tablespoons sherry vinegar or red-wine vinegar
- 1 teaspoon chili powder or 1/2 teaspoon smoked paprika

Directions:
1. Add the asparagus in the frying basket, coat with the oil spray, add the chili powder/paprika, garlic powder and salt on top. Stir well to coat evenly.
2. Place Instant Pot Air Fryer Crisp over kitchen platform. Press Air Fry, set temperature to 400°F and set timer to 5 minutes to preheat. Press "Start" and allow it to preheat for 5 minute.
3. In the inner pot, place the Air Fryer basket. In the basket, add the asparagus mixture.
4. Close the Crisp Lid and press "Air Fry" setting. Set temperature to 400°F and set timer to 10 minutes. Press "Start".
5. Half way down, open the Crisp Lid, shake the basket and close the lid to continue cooking for remaining time.
6. Open the Crisp Lid after cooking time is over. Drizzle with the vinegar on top and serve with your choice of dip or ketchup.

Apple Sweet Chips

Cooking Time: 12 minutes
Serves: 2-3

Ingredients:
- 2 teaspoons sugar
- ½ teaspoon ground cinnamon
- 2 large apples, cored and sliced

Directions:
1. In a bowl, mix the apple pieces with sugar and cinnamon.
2. Place Instant Pot Air Fryer Crisp over kitchen platform. Press Air Fry, set the temperature to 400°F and set the timer to 5 minutes to preheat. Press "Start" and allow it to preheat for 5 minutes.
3. In the inner pot, place the Air Fryer basket. In the basket, add the coated apples. Do not overlap.
4. Close the Crisp Lid and press the "Roast" setting. Set temperature to 350°F and set the timer to 12 minutes. Press "Start."
5. Halfway down, open the Crisp Lid, shake the basket and close the lid to continue cooking for the remaining time.
6. Open the Crisp Lid after cooking time is over. Serve warm.

Creamed Toasted Sticks

Cooking Time: 8 minutes
Serves: 5-6

Ingredients:
- 1/3 cup whole milk
- 1/3 cup heavy cream
- 2 large eggs
- 1/4 teaspoon ground cinnamon
- 3 tablespoon granulated sugar
- 6 thick bread slices cut into 3 parts
- 1/2 teaspoon pure vanilla extract
- Kosher salt and maple syrup to taste

Directions:
1. In a mixing bowl, beat the eggs and add the sugar, milk, cinnamon, and salt; combine well. Coat the bread slices with the mixture.
2. Place Instant Pot Air Fryer Crisp over kitchen platform. Press Air Fry, set the temperature to 400°F and set the timer to 5 minutes to preheat. Press "Start" and allow it to preheat for 5 minutes.
3. In the inner pot, place the Air Fryer basket. Line it with a parchment paper, add the bread slices.
4. Close the Crisp Lid and press the "Air Fry" setting. Set temperature to 370°F and set the timer to 8 minutes. Press "Start."
5. Halfway down, open the Crisp Lid, shake the basket and close the lid to continue cooking for the remaining time.
6. Open the Crisp Lid after cooking time is over. Serve warm with the maple syrup on top.

Spicy Kale Chips

Cooking Time: 5 minutes
Serves: 2-3

Ingredients:
- 1 bunch of Tuscan kale (stems removed and leaves cut into 2-inch pieces)
- 2 tablespoons olive oil
- 1/4 teaspoon crushed red pepper
- 1/4 teaspoon salt
- 1/4 teaspoon paprika
- 1/4 teaspoon garlic powder

Directions:
1. In a mixing bowl, add the olive oil, kale leaves, and spices. Combine the ingredients to mix well with each other.
2. Place Instant Pot Air Fryer Crisp over kitchen platform. Press Air Fry, set the temperature to 400°F and set the timer to 5 minutes to preheat. Press "Start" and allow it to preheat for 5 minutes.
3. In the inner pot, place the Air Fryer basket. In the basket, add the kale mixture.
4. Close the Crisp Lid and press the "Air Fry" setting. Set temperature to 390°F and set the timer to 5 minutes. Press "Start."
5. Halfway down, open the Crisp Lid, shake the basket and close the lid to continue cooking for the remaining time.
6. Open the Crisp Lid after cooking time is over. Season to taste and serve warm.

CHAPTER 9: MOST POPULAR AIR FRYER LID RECIPES

Spiced Cajun Turkey Meatloaf

Cooking Time: 25 minutes   Serves: 6

Ingredients:
- 1½ pounds turkey breasts, ground
- 2 tablespoons butter, at room temperature
- ½ cup scallions, chopped
- ½ sprig of coriander, chopped
- ½ sprig of thyme, chopped
- ½ teaspoon Cajun seasoning
- ⅓ teaspoon ground nutmeg
- ⅓ teaspoon mixed peppercorns, freshly cracked
- ½ teaspoon salt
- ½ cup vegetable stock
- ½ cup seasoned bread crumbs
- 2 eggs, lightly beaten
- 2 teaspoons whole grain mustard
- ⅓ cup tomato ketchup
- Cooking spray

Directions:
1. Melt the butter over moderate heat in a medium saucepan. Add and cook the scallions, coriander, and chopped thyme for 3 minutes until soft.
2. Mix the remaining ingredients except the ketchup in a large bowl. Add the cooked mixture. Toss to combine well.
3. Form the mixture into a meatloaf. Line a parchment paper into the air fryer basket, and spritz with cooking spray. Arrange the meatloaf in the basket.
4. Put the air fryer lid on and cook in the preheated instant pot at 375°F for 20 minutes or until cooked through. Pour the ketchup on top of the meatloaf halfway through the cooking time.
5. Remove the meatloaf from the basket onto a platter. Slice to serve.

Wine-Braised Turkey Breasts

Cooking Time: 35 minutes
Serves: 4

Ingredients:
- ½ pound turkey breasts, boneless, skinless and sliced, rinsed and drained
- Sea salt flakes and cracked black peppercorns, to taste
- ⅓ cup dry white wine
- ½ tablespoon honey
- 1½ tablespoons sesame oil
- 2 tablespoons oyster sauce
- ½ cup plain flour

Directions:
1. Arrange the turkey on a clean work surface. Sprinkle the cracked peppercorns and the sea salt to season. Set aside.
2. Combine well the remaining ingredients except the flour in a large bowl. Dunk the turkey in the mixture. Refrigerate to marinate for no less than 1 hour.
3. Discard the marinade. Dredge the turkey slices in the plain flour in a separate bowl, then arrange the turkey in the air fryer basket.
4. Put the air fryer lid on and cook in batches in the preheated instant pot at 375°F for 16 minutes, flipping the turkey slices once during cooking time.
5. Transfer the cooked turkey breasts to a platter and serve.

Savory Sage and Lime Wings

Cooking Time: 25 minutes
Serves: 4

Ingredients:
- 2 heaping tablespoons sage, chopped
- ⅓ cup fresh lime juice
- ½ pound turkey wings, cut into smaller pieces
- ⅓ teaspoon mustard powder
- ½ tablespoon corn flour
- ½ teaspoon seasoned salt
- ½ teaspoon garlic powder
- ½ tablespoon fresh parsley, chopped
- 1 teaspoon onion powder
- 1 teaspoon cracked black or white peppercorns
- Cooking spray

Directions:
1. In a large bowl, put the sage, lime juice, turkey wings, mustard powder, corn flour, salt, garlic powder, parsley, onion powder, and peppercorns. Stir to combine well. Marinate in the freezer for one hour.
2. Spritz a 6×6×2-inch baking pan with cooking spray. Remove the bowl from the freezer and pour the mixture in the pan. Arrange the pan in the air fryer basket.
3. Put the air fryer lid on and bake in the preheated instant pot at 350°F for 20 minutes or until cooked through.
4. Remove the pan from the basket and serve the wings on a large platter.

Baked Festive Turkey Drumsticks

Cooking Time: 35 minutes
Serves: 6

Ingredients:
- 3 turkey drumsticks
- 2 teaspoons olive oil
- ½ cup tamari sauce or soy sauce
- ⅓ cup apple cider vinegar
- ½ tablespoon Dijon mustard
- 2 sprigs rosemary, chopped
- ½ teaspoon smoked cayenne pepper
- Kosher salt and ground black pepper, to taste
- 3 Gala apples, cored and diced

Directions:
1. In a bowl, toss the drumsticks with olive oil, tamari, and apple cider vinegar. Refrigerate to marinate for at least 3 hours or overnight.
2. Transfer the drumsticks to a large bowl. Sprinkle the Dijon mustard, rosemary, smoked cayenne pepper, black pepper, and salt on top.
3. Arrange the marinated drumsticks in a 6×6×2-inch baking pan, then top with the apple dices. Place the pan in the air fryer basket.
4. Put the air fryer lid on and cook in batches in the preheated instant pot at 325°F for 22 minutes, flipping the turkey drumsticks when the lid screen indicates 'TURN FOOD' halfway through the cooking time.
5. Remove from the basket and serve on a large platter.

CPSIA information can be obtained
at www.ICGtesting.com
Printed in the USA
BVHW081438210820
586989BV00020B/222